50

Showdown in Seville
KASPAROV-KARPOV IV

RAYMOND KEENE
DAVID GOODMAN
DAVID SPANIER

D0829561

Collier Books
Macmillan Publishing Company
New York

Collier Books
Macmillan Publishing Company
866 Third Avenue, New York, NY 10022
Collier Macmillan Canada, Inc.

ISBN 0-02-044131-2

Macmillan books are available at special discounts for bulk purchases for sales promotions, premiums, fund-raising, or educational use. For details, contact:

Special Sales Director
Macmillan Publishing Company
866 Third Avenue
New York, NY 10022

10 9 8 7 6 5 4 3 2 1

Printed in Great Britain

Acknowledgments

The authors express their thanks to many people, in chess and beyond it. In particular, they would like to mention Denis Teyssou of Agence France Presse for game times; Andrew Whiteley and Paul Lamford for editorial back-up; many friendly couriers from Seville and helpers in London; a bevy of masters at the ringside, most of whom disagreed with each other; a number of journalists, in particular Jon Tisdall of Reuters, Leontxo García of *El País* and Fernando Urias of *Diario 16*; and not least Spanish tournament officials, notably Carmen Otero, who kept the press room open late into the night.

The text is, of course, a collective effort; but in case any readers want to apportion praise or blame, it would be fair to say that Keene provided most of the analysis, Goodman the colour and Spanier the politics.

Move Times

Whenever possible the cumulative number of minutes used is shown in italics after a move. These times were displayed by a computer clock linked to the board and activated by White's playing his first move, hence a discrepancy with chess-clock time may occur in the early stages of the game if White's clock was allowed to run before the start.

The time limit is 40 moves in the first 150 minutes and 16 moves per 60 minutes thereafter.

1 Introduction

All is not well in the world of chess. The stand-up row between Gary Kasparov and Florencio Campomanes, president of FIDE, the International Chess Federation, is hardly a secret. It began during the aborted world championship match in Moscow of September 1984 to February 1985, when it looked as if Kasparov would never win the title which he eventually prised from Karpov's grasp nine months later. It has flared up, again and again, in various parts of the world, during the past three years, culminating in the formation of the break-away Grandmasters Association in Brussels on 27 April 1987.

Such a breach between the world champion and the other top players on one side, and the official responsible for organising the world chess championship on the other, is unprecedented. It is also, obviously enough, undesirable, in the diversion of energies it implies, even if competition itself is healthy. Whether the two sides will reach a rapprochement or go their separate ways is the central issue in chess today.

However many times the charges and counter-charges are repeated – Kasparov's conviction that Campomanes stopped the original match in Moscow to save Karpov from defeat, as against Campomanes' own claim that he intervened to spare the players further ordeal after 48 games – neither side has been able, in the nature of things, to prove its case entirely. Nevertheless, chess players around the world judged that the sudden ending of that match, whatever the reasons given, marked a dreadful day in the history of chess, which must never be repeated.

The significance of this row, highlighted by a clash of personalities as well as of principle, is that it launched a personal feud which, as events have unfolded, has grown more bitter and fanned outwards to involve international chess as a whole. Kasparov, clearly, no longer trusts the FIDE president to act fairly. Campomanes, as he once put it, is determined "to teach that young man who is boss".

1

In chess terms, the political events of the past three years may be seen as attack (Kasparov), counter-attack (Campomanes) and flanking movement (Kasparov), with the result still unclear.

It was the widespread disaffection with Campomanes' style of leadership, a style which his critics termed egocentric and dictatorial, which persuaded a group of leading chess players, led by Kasparov, to oppose his re-election as president of FIDE in December 1986. The candidate they chose was a Brazilian, Lincoln Lucena. Running on the same ticket, for the post of secretary, was the English grandmaster and chess writer Raymond Keene (one of the authors of this book), who by reason of his wide experience of international chess was seen, in practice, as the real alternative to Campomanes. The rival campaign failed. The story, fascinating in itself, is important because it was this attempt which led directly to the establishment of the Grandmasters Association (GMA) – the first president of which, of course, is none other than "that young man" himself.

The FIDE elections took place, as is usual, during the olympiad, which was held, not as usual, in the Arab world, in the tiny sheikhdom of Dubai. It was an excellent thing, no doubt, to hold the biennial olympiad in a new country, and in a part of the world, moreover, which had contributed during the middle ages so much to the development of chess. But there were various aspects of the event which gave cause for international concern.

The most immediate was the exclusion of Israel. Understandable as it might well be that an Arab country would not want to play host to an Israeli team, the fact is that the olympiad is open to all. That is the *raison d'être* of the event. So if the FIDE motto, *Gens Una Sumus* (We Are One People), meant anything, then FIDE should surely have turned down any offer to hold the chess olympiad in a country which – for reasons of its own – could not or would not willingly issue visas to chess players of another member country.

But FIDE did not turn down the offer from Dubai; it gave its approval. A deal was struck, behind the scenes, whereby the Israeli Chess Federation, though not formally barred from taking part, was persuaded, perhaps in the interest of "good sportsmanship", not to press its case. By the time the issue came to be discussed in the open, it was too late. In protest at what had happened, three important chess playing countries, Holland, Norway and Denmark, decided to boycott the

olympiad (as did one British grandmaster). The United States, after much heated argument, chose to send its team, on the express condition that American officials should secure an amendment to the rules, to ensure that Israel's exclusion should never be countenanced again.*
All this was in a sense a side issue, though it cast a distinctly bad odour over the chosen venue from the outset.

Of far greater significance was the number of countries which did send teams, a record 106 out of a membership of around 124. An admirable turn-out! How did Dubai manage to attract so many? The answer was that the president of FIDE was able to offer a large number of them free air travel. The organisers in Dubai, where considerations of finance were evidently no problem, produced the funds. Campomanes himself distributed the invitations. "A wonderful idea", according to the spokesman of the olympiad organising committee, one Ahmed Abdullah Abu Hussein. "We admit before the world and we say without hesitation that the idea was his."

The suspicion – it could be no more than that – in the rival camp to Campomanes was that countries benefiting from such largesse would be likely, if not virtually certain, to cast their votes for the man who had so helped them. Why not? A sense of gratitude in chess players burns no less ardently, it may be presumed, than among other mortals. A return ticket to Dubai, plus two or three weeks' free stay in a five-star hotel, might be a certain inducement, might it not, towards showing appreciation. The list of countries which received such hospitality** was not confined to those

---

* In a review of Standing Order to Statute 1.2 the following wording was agreed: (1) FIDE events (competitions, congresses, meetings) may be hosted only by federations in whose countries free access is generally assured to representatives of all federations. (2) The General Assembly may make exceptions for reasons of state war or severe violence between countries only on a three quarters majority vote.

** Algeria, Andorra, Angola, Argentina, Bahamas, Bangladesh, Barbados, Bolivia, Botswana, British Virgin Islands, Chile, China, Colombia, Costa Rica, Cuba, Cyprus, Dominica, Egypt, Fiji, Gambia, Greece, Guatemala, Guyana, Haiti, Honduras, India, Iraq, Italy, Jamaica, Jordan, Kenya, Lebanon, Mali, Malta, Mauritius, Mauritania, Mexico, Morocco, New Guinea, Nicaragua, Nigeria, Pakistan, Panama, Paraguay, Peru, Puerto Rico, Philippines, the PLO(!), San Marino, Senegal, Seychelles, Singapore, Spain, Sri Lanka, Sudan, Syria, Thailand, Trinidad & Tobago, Tunisia, Turkey, Uruguay, Uganda, Venezuela, Zambia, Zaire.

3

from the developing world, which might be most in need; two or three European countries were also in the receiving line. While two or three other countries, believed to oppose Campomanes, like Bermuda, Hong Kong and Zimbabwe, were not. The total cost was put at around $750,000.

Campomanes, an experienced campaigner, did not deign to dignify such accusations from his critics by denying them. He had no need to. He had a long record of helping countries of the developing world get their chess going – by supplying equipment and books, organising visits by masters, and so on. He had indeed based his first campaign for election as president back in 1982 on these countries' support. He was respected and admired by very many of them for the contribution he had made, long before the issue of free tickets to Dubai came up.

In his first tilt at the presidency, Campo (as he is universally known) had the advantage of open-ended backing from his own country. In the Philippines chess is second in popularity only to basketball. His election as president of FIDE, displacing a good but uncharismatic incumbent, Fridrik Olafsson of Iceland, was received back home as a tribute to President Marcos' leadership; and as an adroit politician – plastering photos of himself on the walls, distributing colourful brochures depicting his travels on behalf of chess in the third world, and handing out Philippine cigars on the day of the vote – Campo had, perhaps, modelled himself on Marcos. His election was a triumph achieved with more razmatazz than chess had seen in many a long day. It also signified a swing from the old world, where Europe had long dominated FIDE, to the new, to the expanding swathe of developing nations, at whose head he stood as flag-waver.

But this time, in the election in Dubai, Campo was out on his own, the Marcos connection gone. He was faced, moreover, by a challenger who though not well known in the world of chess did have the unique advantage of endorsement by the current world champion – a young man in a hurry, brimming with new ideas and energy, not just a celebrity at the chessboard but a Soviet-style pop star. He was on record, at home and abroad, in outspoken condemnation of Campomanes' conduct of FIDE. "Chess has been rocked by scandals which must now come to an end," Kasparov told the local paper on arrival in Dubai. "This autocratic style of leadership has harmed everyone. He has had four years to make his own chess world, and the result is bad."

4

Campomanes was well aware of European dislike of his self-promotion, of criticism of his use of FIDE funds, of the continuing resentment, not just from Kasparov, at his decision to stop the Moscow match, which had clogged up and delayed the world championship cycle. On top of this, he had to take account of Lucena's globe-trotting to solicit votes, especially in his native Latin America – he claimed that Lucena was spending a fortune on his campaign travels. So this was going to be an altogether different and tougher election. How was he going to win it?

Campo, as everyone in chess recognized, had a 2600 rating as a politician. Quick, fluent, sharp, on first-name terms with all the players and delegates, he was a capable speaker and a ready listener. He already had the votes, well in hand, from his years in office. The real question was whether he could hang on to them. The decision to hold the election in Dubai was certainly highly advantageous; it took the election out of the old European frame, away from his most persistent critics, and set it in a new context. The Arab countries' votes, an important bloc, could naturally be expected to follow. Africa and Asia, thanks to his own globe-trotting, were more or less in the bag. Latin America was obviously his opponent's strong suit; but not even Lucena's warmest admirers could say that he was a strong candidate. He was kind, amiable, well intentioned, yes – but no public speaker, no vote-winner.

It looked as if the election was going to turn on the Soviet Union's vote. Whichever of the two candidates the Soviet Chess Federation backed – given that its allies of the Eastern bloc would certainly follow the Soviet lead – would carry the day, quite easily. According to speculation in the lobbies of the Hilton Hotel where the delegates were gathered, Moscow was still undecided.

This was the hopeful view in the Lucena camp, where an experienced campaign organiser, former Scottish international David Levy – the man who had won a famous bet against the champions of artificial intelligence in academe that they couldn't design a computer chess program to beat him in the decade to 1980 – was in charge of the counter-attack. As things were, he put Lucena's chances in the election at somewhat less than evens. But he calculated that their man might be catching up and could even just pip Campo when it came to the vote at the end of the week, thanks to one extraordinarily powerful piece they were now bringing into play – a sort of secret weapon.

Gary Kasparov, naturally, was playing top board for the Soviet Union in the olympiad. But that did not prevent him from throwing himself into the election campaign, head first. He was, he is, a new breed of Soviet chess player, not afraid to speak his mind, unencumbered by the weight of tradition which had made so many of his elders either toe the official line or jump over it to a freer life in the West. From the start he had been completely open about his dislike and resentment of Campomanes' style, of his conduct of the world championship in particular and of FIDE in general. He wanted him out.

Each night, when the day's play in the olympiad was over, the young world champion got involved directly in the campaign. In secluded meetings in his hotel suite, delegates were invited up for a chat and a late night drink. Every national chess federation which it was thought had not irrevocably committed its vote to Campo, or which might still have an open mind, was invited.

What a treat for these functionaries of the royal game! To meet the superstar of chess, eyes beetling under his bushy eyebrows, dressed in a white sweater and jeans, in such a relaxed setting, and to hear him hold forth so strongly. Kasparov did not go in for crude electioneering (he was evidently somewhat underwhelmed by the alternative candidate). On the contrary, he simply set out his own position – that the way the world championship in Moscow had been aborted had been wrong, that FIDE was being run in an autocratic way which ignored the feelings of himself and other leading players, that the benefits being held out to the developing countries (perhaps some of his listeners facing him in their armchairs gave a thought to their free air fares and hotel rooms) were illusory. More practical help could be given them via coaching and visits by top grandmasters, Kasparov included, and more prudent budgeting of FIDE funds. Such was Kasparov's election speech. He did not suggest they should vote for Lucena – who was of course present in the room. He simply invited them to draw the obvious conclusion: time for a change.

These nightly meetings represented a big effort of time and energy by Kasparov, when he might have been expected to conserve all his creative talents for playing for his country each day. In fact the Soviet Union was at that point trailing badly. At the board Kasparov slipped only once, in pressing too hard for the win in a clearly drawn position against US champion Yasser Seirawan. He still won the gold medal on top board, so his heavy electioneering cannot be said to have harmed his play. Indeed the Soviet Union in the end managed to pip England for the gold medal for the second olympiad running.

Kasparov, however, had a "hole" in his position, a weak point. Bold and outspoken as he might be, he had little or no experience of the internal rivalries and machinations that determine who is who in Soviet sport or who has real power in the chess federation. Many members of the old guard were jealous of his meteoric rise to the top and of his arrogant assumption that he could say and do as he pleased – a free-wheeling style of life inconceivable in former times, when the "authorities" kept chess players on a very tight rein. No foreign travel without official approval, no free and easy statements to the press, above all no criticism of Soviet players – and this kid from Azerbaijan was getting away with all of this!

Perhaps Kasparov was a shade naive, understandably so, when it came to politics. At any rate, for all his outward confidence, he did not know, when it came to the crunch, if he could deliver his own country's vote, notwithstanding his popularity in the Soviet Union as the most exciting chess player since Bobby Fischer.

In Lucena's camp, hopes were rising. A head count indicated that they were closing on Campo and might even be inching ahead. How would the Russians make up their minds, finally? There had been changes in the membership of the Soviet Chess Federation since Kasparov displaced Karpov, but not all the way through. Most of the membership were thought to be Karpov supporters, which implied playing safe, holding the status quo, resisting change. The head of the Soviet delegation for most of the time in Dubai was Dr Nikolai Krogius, a distinguished player in his own right, but an establishment figure. There were frantic telephone calls from Dubai to Moscow ahead of the arrival of the newly elected president, Alexander Chikvaidze, but no assurances about voting intentions.

The Russians like to be winners. Their most likely course – assuming the decision had not already been taken in Moscow – was that they would sound out the mood of the FIDE Assembly and then plump for whichever candidate looked like being the winner – rather than risk winding up on the losing side. Campo had started favourite; and for all his reputation as a wheeler and dealer (he had given the Russians a terrible time in forcing the replay of the candidates in 1983) he was, after all, a known quantity, the president in office. After the way he had intervened in stopping the Moscow match, the Russians – or the Karpov clique which had approved of his decision to stop the match – might feel in his debt. And in the end, when it came to the vote, what sort of a president would a man like Lucena really make, however amiable?

Whatever the precise reasons which led up to their decision, two days before the vote word got around Dubai that the Russians had made up their minds. The Soviet delegation was going to back Campomanes. The Eastern bloc countries would vote with it. Suddenly Lucena's candidacy looked ridiculous – he was going to lose by a mile. Frantic consultations were held up in Lucena's suite. Not surprisingly, he decided to stand down "in the interests of unity". Next day Campo was re-elected unopposed. It was a personal triumph and in FIDE terms a great victory.

But not, as events were rapidly to show, a total victory. Kasparov's all-out frontal attack (typical of his style in chess) had been repulsed so far as the election was concerned, but he was nowhere near losing the game. His plan was to outflank FIDE by securing the players' aims in a totally different way. The Grandmasters' Association, which would never have got off the ground if Campo had lost the election, was the chosen method.

For all his campaigning against him, Kasparov had no doubt foreseen Campomanes' success a long way off. He had begun sounding out a few of the top players as he saw them in the hotel lobby or the restaurant well before the election. Finally he asked a select group to come up to his suite. "Gary was very determined – it was more like an order," one of them recalls. Also present was a man who, though a self-confessed addict of chess, was not a player himself. He was a Dutch-born financier named Bessel Kok. His was a new name in international chess and potentially an important one.

The Grandmasters' Association owed its start to his generosity. As chief executive of SWIFT (Society for Worldwide Interbank Telecommunications) in Brussels, Bessel Kok had long been keen to give his company a more public profile. Chess seemed an ideal medium. The first SWIFT tournament in Brussels in 1986 had been a resounding success, not least for the efficient way it was run.

"My interest in chess has always been there," Kok said, explaining his sudden arrival on the scene, "but I never saw an opportunity to do anything about it." After the first tournament, which was a hit with the players, Kok met Kasparov and persuaded him to play alongside both Karpov and Korchnoi in the second tournament. Significantly, his approach to chess sponsorship is "for the players and by the players".

Given his growing involvement in chess, it was a logical next move to fly to Dubai. It was there that Kasparov invited him to help in launching the GMA. "What I liked in it was that it was a spontaneous move," Kok recalled in *New in Chess* No 4, 1987. "You cannot create associations by preparing them six months in advance. It was an outburst . . . they all came to this famous meeting that started at midnight in Kasparov's suite in the Hilton Hotel. And they asked me if I could be, I don't know the exact word, their *parrain*, their godfather."

When they were all there, Kasparov set out his ideas for a new kind of players' organisation – there was no name for it yet – to look after the players' interests. The meeting lasted two or three hours. John Nunn was then deputed to type out the various proposals which were to form the basis of the GMA. Kok set only one condition, he says: the chess players had to give him their word that they would work at the new project in a totally disciplined way.

Kasparov was duly nominated president of the GMA and his arch-rival Karpov vice president – a notable declaration of solidarity on his part. Karpov's reputation had been very badly hurt by the allegations that Campomanes' favouritism 'saved his skin' in the Moscow match ("President Karpovmanes" in Spassky's quip). By supporting the GMA in this public way Karpov was now unequivocally throwing in his lot with the new wave in international chess. Other members of the GMA Council were Ljubomir Ljubojević (Yugoslavia), John Nunn (England), Lajos Portisch (Hungary), Yasser Seirawan (United States) and Jan Timman (Netherlands). Nunn shortly stood down because of his other commitments, being replaced by Bent Larsen (Denmark).

Kasparov sprang the news on an embarrassed and angry Campomanes in a public announcement in the Hilton lobby, immediately after the olympiad prizegiving.

The prime aim of the GMA is to stage a world cup consisting of six major tournaments, to be held in different cities over a two year period, starting in 1988-89. The essential condition for success is, of course, commercial sponsorship, which seems likely to be forthcoming despite the relatively high cost – say $250,000 per tournament. Bessel Kok himself will back one event, in Brussels – which he would like to see become the chess capital of the world.

24 grandmasters will compete for the world cup, the winner being the player who scores most points – rather like the motor racing grands prix. (Each of the 24 players will compete in four out of six tournaments of sixteen players each.) The third year of the cycle, 1990, will be occupied by the run-up to the world championship. This is exclusively FIDE's responsibility. All the players involved will then be concentrating their energies on the interzonals and the candidates matches. After the next world championship, the world cup would then start again in 1991 – such is the ambitious programme envisaged by the GMA. Aware, however, of their "elitist image", Kok insists that the world cup is only one of the objectives. The organisation is intended to be democratic, with the aim of improving professional chess for all players.

There was a lot of talk about co-operation with FIDE. No one was against it, if it could be done; and Campo was invited to the first meeting of the founding members, which took place in Bessel Kok's offices in Brussels early in the new year. But agreement could not be reached. The players were determined to run their own show. The articles of association were finally agreed at a second meeting, in April 1987, and the GMA was officially launched.

Kok deprecates suggestions that he has any aspiration to get involved in FIDE. "My answer has been that I have a fantastic job to which I am fully devoted and I would like to continue that." He adds, delphically, that "at the moment the answer is no. However, if the circumstances change we can always see . . ." He continues to maintain that a lot of things must change in FIDE. (The only thing that has changed so far is that the former Players' Council is obviously defunct.)

The first board meeting of the GMA was held in Bilbao in August. In return for the city meeting the visitors' costs, Kasparov, Karpov, Timman, Ljubojević, Portisch, Larsen, Nunn and Lubosh Kavalek (United States, appointed GMA organisational director) gave a simultaneous display for 200 local schoolchildren. The split with FIDE over the way it set rules and tournament conditions widened. The players at the board meeting issued a communiqué to "stress the fact that as professional chess players they are best qualified and entitled to make recommendations affecting their professional careers . . . continuing to ignore our recommendations can only be viewed as an attempt to thwart the efforts of the GMA."

Clearly, the GMA has yet to prove itself, by organising tournaments of high quality which attract public interest and TV coverage. If so, the world cup could make an extremely valuable contribution to popularising chess, as well as enriching the top players.

Meanwhile, Campomanes continued with the preparations for the world championship. Five towns put in bids to stage the present event, the fourth K v K encounter in three years. Seattle (Seirawan's home town) and Sochi on the Black Sea both offered the minimum one million Swiss Francs in prize money, Madrid two million, Dubai itself bid 2.25 million and Seville 2.8 million (about £1.17 million or $1.9 million). Kasparov had made it clear he was not going to play the world championship in Dubai, in any circumstances, so it was perhaps just as well that Dubai's bid was not the highest. The players could not agree on the choice of venue, and in these circumstances the new FIDE rules stipulated that the match be awarded to Seville as the highest bidder. Thus the world championship returned to one of the oldest chess playing countries in Europe.

So far as FIDE coming to terms with the GMA goes, the prospects do not look encouraging. In the early days, with acrimonious letters flying back and forth between Lucerne (FIDE) and Brussels (GMA), mutual suspicion blocked any chance of a rapprochement. And that is how the position remained up to the start of this world championship in Seville.

2 Barbs in Seville

The players' delegations arrived in Seville on the same flight from Moscow, but left the plane by separate exits. Kasparov and Karpov declined to be photographed together on the tarmac. Everyone knew, in any case, that their personal relations were only a degree above freezing point.

The latest development was the publication, in English, of Kasparov's no-holds-barred autobiography *Child of Change*, timed to coincide with the start of the world championship. This book, published in Spain as *Hijo del Cambio*, was a long yelp of protest against what Kasparov claimed was the official Soviet conspiracy, instigated by Karpov, to hold him back and prevent him becoming world champion. It is an extraordinarily outspoken – or, if you like, courageous – book, inconceivable in the old days before *glasnost* became the Kremlin watchword. Karpov, cast as conformist, conservative and pro-Campomanes, comes out of it very badly.

The climax of *Child of Change*, as expected, was a detailed and well-documented critique of Campomanes' decision to stop Kasparov's first world championship duel with Karpov. The book also confirmed that in his time of trouble Kasparov approached a politburo member, Geidar Aliev from his native Azerbaijan, to help unblock the way ahead; which he did. (Aliev left the leadership in October 1987 for "health" reasons.)

Clearly, the principal interest in the pre-match press conference lay in what Karpov might have to say in response to all this. Many people, players and journalists alike, expected that the former champion would be spurred on to speak out in his defence; it was, evidently, his turn to move.

The organisers announced that Kasparov intended to give two news conferences, while Karpov would have his own show the following morning, the day of the opening ceremony. (A sign of how the times are changing: Kasparov had a prior engagement at the Alfonso XIII Hotel to film a Spanish television commercial for Schweppes tonic water, the first ever TV ad to feature a Soviet citizen.)

For his opening press conference, in the high-tech Sevilla Sol Hotel, Kasparov was flanked by friends and colleagues of the new Grandmasters Association: Karpov himself (co-vice president with Jan Timman), Ulf Andersson and the GMA "godfather" Bessel Kok. Kasparov announced an ambitious programme of tournaments for the forthcoming world cup: Brussels, Bilbao and Reykjavik in 1988, Barcelona, Rotterdam and Skelleftea (northern Sweden) for 1989. As Karpov left the platform, the two protagonists shook hands, though so fleetingly it would have taken a photo-finish camera to catch the moment. The others returned to the audience and the main event got under way.

Speaking mainly in Russian, which was translated first into Spanish and then English, Kasparov said he felt "very confident" of his chances in the match, but shied away from making predictions. He also explained that he saw his relationship with Karpov as a two-sided affair: they were working together in the GMA; but their rivalry in the world championship continued, exacerbated by their sharply opposing approaches to chess. "I hope the former will prevail, but I cannot guarantee it," he said.

After an hour's break, the proceedings resumed in the ornate Alfonso XIII for a more political news conference, designed to promote *Hijo del Cambio*. It was a noisy and confused occasion, though the message was clear enough: Kasparov's conviction that he would never have become world champion without the irreversible changes in Soviet life instituted by Mikhail Gorbachov under *glasnost*. (Or, as he expressed it later, "Now no one can tell Gary Kasparov to shut his mouth.")

If he was on slightly shakier ground in explaining to the international press how it was that his autobiography was not being published in a Russian edition, he carried it off. "This is not for the reasons that many people might think . . . The purpose of the book is to explain chess matters to people in the West. There may come a time when I write a Soviet version, but it would be in a different form."

Karpov's news conference next morning at the Sevilla Sol was much better organised. He, too, expressed his confidence about his chances in the match. A few preliminaries were spent on the GMA, with Bessel Kok repeating the statements made the day before – notably that the GMA was not meant to be "elitist" – while demonstrating, in his godfatherly way, Karpov's personal commitment to the success of the new body.

The conference then moved on to the real issue in hand: Kasparov's personal indictment of Karpov. After an opening question about Karpov's recent second marriage (to Natasha Bulanova, the tall blonde lady who accompanied him during the Leningrad leg of the 1986 contest and was now in Seville as his wife) the meeting got down to brass tacks. Karpov, as befits a former world champion, had a prepared variation, and a pretty sharp one at that. His charge was that Kasparov had been "wobbly" with the truth.

Kasparov had received financial support at every stage of his career and was the most privileged player not only in the Soviet Union but in the whole world, Karpov roundly declared. As a youngster, he had even got a special fee for his mother to act as his coach. "I am not going into all the dirty details," Karpov said. "I just want to mention one or two facts that Kasparov has conveniently forgotten in his attack on me. Where else could he have got conditions like he has in the whole world?"

In particular, Karpov disputed Kasparov's version of the events surrounding the aborted semi-final of the Candidates against Korchnoi in Pasadena in 1983. His own role in the affair, he said, had been to try and rescue the situation. He was likewise extremely sceptical about Kasparov's claim that Yevgeny Vladimirov had been dismissed by Kasparov from his entourage for passing on "secret analysis" to Karpov's camp. Karpov read out a statement from the man he said Kasparov had described as his "guru", Tofik Dadashev, a psychologist who worked with Kasparov during the Leningrad part of the match. The implication given was that all his talk of conspiracy was simply a desperate *post facto* explanation by Kasparov for his three losses in a row in Leningrad.

All in all, Karpov sounded dangerously cool and collected. If the press conferences were to be regarded as a pre-match war of nerves, the challenger was so far the winner on points. He did not, however, attempt to refute Kasparov's basic charge about the stopping of the first match.

In the evening everyone repaired to Seville's casino-like opera house, the Teatro Lope de Vega, elegantly restored for the match in crimson, cream and gold. Workmen were still engaged throughout the weekend in painting and decorating and wiring the stage for the grand opening. A succession of worthy speeches by Campomanes and other dignitaries put the world chess championship in perspective: old men presiding over a young men's battle. In the draw for colours for the opening game, Karpov drew White.

GAME ONE, 12 October

A large crowd gathered at the Lope de Vega Theatre for the players' arrival. Kasparov waited inside his car for several minutes, apparently looking over some last minute notes, before being whisked through his door (marked with a black pawn) into the theatre. Karpov arrived on stage a minute later.

For Seville, the championship was a sporting curtain-raiser to the 1992 World Fair, commemorating the 500th anniversary of Columbus's voyage of discovery to the new world. In a gesture to the hosts, the players had agreed to play with elaborately castellated rooks, modelled on Seville's most celebrated landmark, the Torre del Oro. They rejected Spanish-style knights, however, as too ornate. The play was relayed to video screens set up all around the building via the Intelligent Chess Board system first used in the London match.

After a polite handshake, the fourth K v K duel began. Boris Spassky, who had in his time been both challenger and defending champion, offered the opinion that Kasparov had expended too much time and energy before the match on non-chess matters, while Karpov was enjoying newly married life. He predicted that Karpov would hold the advantage at the start of the match.

Karpov-Kasparov
Neo-Grünfeld Defence

| 1 | d4 | 00 | ♘f6 | 00 |
| 2 | c4 | 00 | g6 | 01 |

Kasparov throws down the gauntlet, boldly showing that he is prepared to resume the theoretical dispute of games 17 and 19 from last year's match.

| 3 | g3 | 04 | | |

Karpov chose this quiet continuation in games 3 and 13 last time, and also at SWIFT in the "century game" earlier this year. Of course, 3 ♘c3 leads to the critical regions of the opening's theory battle.

| 3 | ... | | c6 | 01 |
| 4 | ♘f3 | 04 | ♗g7 | 02 |

5	♗g2	05	d5	03
6	cd	05	cd	03
7	♘c3	06	0-0	04
8	♘e5	06	e6	04
9	0-0	07	♘fd7	05
10	f4	08	♘c6	06

10 ... f6 11 ♘f3 ♘c6 12 ♗e3 ♘b6 13 ♗f2 was slightly more comfortable for White in Karpov-Kasparov, Leningrad (13) 1986. Kasparov-Nunn, Brussels OHRA 1986, went 10 ... ♘xe5 11 fe ♘c6 12 e4!.

11	♗e3	09	♘b6	07
12	♗f2	11	♗d7	09
13	e4	25	♘e7	14

14 ♘xd7! *33*

An innovation, and a good one. Andersson-Hulak, Wijk aan Zee 1987, saw scant progress for White after 14 a4 de 15 ♘xe4 ♗c6 16 a5 ♘bd5 17 ♕b3 ♖b8. Karpov's concept is to gain space, even at the price of relieving Black of his inferior bishop.

14	...		♕xd7	16
15	e5	33	♖fc8	28

16 ♖c1? *50*

Here or on the next move White could have launched a dangerous attack by playing g4 with the plan of f5. Instead, the challenger starts quiet manoeuvres which indicate that he was not truly interested in a fight in this opening game.

One likely continuation after the immediate 16 g4 is 16 ... ♘c4 17 ♕e2 b5 18 ♗h4, suggested by American GM Max Dlugy, though IM Jon Tisdall's idea of 18 ... b4 19 ♘d1 ♘c6 20 ♕d3 ♗f8 21 ♔h1 b3 22 a3 (if 22 ab ♘4a5 followed by 23 ... ♖ab8) 22 ... a5 to play ... ♕a7-a6 seems to be OK for Black. Another way for White to proceed is 18 ♗h3 instead of 18 ♗h4 in the above variation. For example, 18 ... b4 19 ♘d1 ♘c6 20 b3 ♘a3 21 ♘b2, but Black stands well after 21 ... a6, to answer 22 ♘d3 with ... ♘b5 hitting the d-pawn.

16	...		♗f8	62
17	♗f3?!	56		

In the press room, grandmasters

Eduard Gufeld and Miguel Najdorf criticised this move. Now, they suggested, was surely the right time for g4. Tisdall analysed some complicated variations that follow 17 g4 ♖c6 18 ♗h4 ♖ac8 19 f5 ef 20 ♕f3, but 20 ... ♖c4 21 ♖cd1 ♘c6 holds for Black. Later, though, he discovered an extremely dangerous exchange sacrifice with 20 ♗xe7 instead of 20 ♕f3. After the natural moves 20 ... ♗xe7 21 gf ♗g5 White can play 22 f6!? ♗xc1 23 ♕xc1 ♔h8 24 ♕h6 ♖g8 25 ♗h3 ♕d8 26 ♖f4 ♕f8 27 ♕g5. Although Black can avert any direct mating attack he is badly tied up.

17	...		♖c7	82
18	b3	79	♖ac8	86
19	♕d2	81	♘c6	89

Preventing 20 ♘b5, viz 20 ... ♘xe5 21 ♖xc7 ♘xf3+ 22 ♔g2 ♘xd2 23 ♖xd7 ♘xd7, or 21 fe ♕xb5.

20	♕b2	85	a6	91
21	♗e2	91	♕e7	105
22	♘b1	100		

Passive, but Black was threatening ... ♕a3.

22	...		♘b4	107

Now Black has threats on the c-file. A pattern for a draw by repetition is emerging.

23	♘c3	106	♘c6	108
24	♘b1	110	♘b4	110
25	♖c5	110	♘d7	114
26	♖xc7	110	♖xc7	114
27	♘c3	110	♘c6	115

Again with the idea of ... ♕a3.

28	♘b1	132	♘b4	117
29	♘c3	141	♘c6	128
30	♘b1	141		

Kasparov now announced he would play 30 ... ♘b4 and claimed a draw by repetition of position.

Draw

Kasparov	½
Karpov	½

GAME TWO, 14 October

It was scarcely to be believed . . .

After playing his 26th move in a complicated time scramble Kasparov failed to punch his clock. For an agonising two minutes and forty seconds the title-holder's team looked on helplessly as their man's time ebbed relentlessly away.

In the press room, experts jostled each other for the best views of the video screens. "He forget, he forget", screamed Soviet grandmaster Gufeld in English. In the hall hushed spectators wondered if Kasparov would actually lose on time.

With less than a minute to go, Kasparov's eyes finally focused on the clock. He punched the button, shook his head and glared at Karpov. But the challenger never wavered. As Kasparov struggled frantically to make the control, Karpov closed in with a killing kingside mating attack. When Kasparov resigned, he was so short of time that some observers mistakenly thought his flag had fallen.

It is one thing to lose your first game with White – quite another to crash to earth like this. In Spassky's vivid phrase, Kasparov looked as though the entire Lope de Vega Theatre had fallen down on him at the end of the game.

The high drama that preceded Karpov's devastating pyschological victory followed a zig-zag tactical struggle which featured a seemingly endless series of number-crunching variations. The first surprise came right at the start. Kasparov opened with a main line English, but it was Karpov who weighed in with a mighty novelty on move nine. This left Kasparov pondering for a marathon eighty minutes over his reply.

In the ensuing complications experienced grandmasters were forced to change their evaluation of the position move by move. One minute they said Kasparov stood better, moments later it was Karpov. In the confusion Kasparov missed one possibility that may well have led to a win.

As the dust settled, there could be no doubt that Karpov was in control. White's defensive resources were systematically stripped away as Kasparov, visibly shaken, searched desperately for the best defence. It was then that he failed to hit the clock.

When the cliff-hanging tension had finally been resolved, experts wondered if anything similar had ever happened before in a world title contest. Ironically, a similar fate befell Kasparov's mentor Mikhail Botvinnik during his 1958 championship duel with Vasily Smyslov. In the 15th game, Botvinnik had only two moves to make in an easily winning position, but he pondered on a move until his clock fell. "I simply forgot there was a clock," he later explained.

Adding to the unusual flavour of the whole affair, the chief arbiter Geurt Gijssen of Holland told reporters after the game that a black cat – an ambiguous symbol, bad luck in some superstitions, good luck in others – had been running around under the stage during the latter part of the game, its scratching and mewing possibly audible to the players.

When a Spanish journalist could describe Kasparov's errors as caused by "childish carelessness", it confirmed the general view that Kasparov's nerves were not exactly steady. So full marks to Boris Spassky. Not only had he correctly predicted the psychological state of both players at the beginning of the match, it was he who told his audience after move 17, "Today we are going to see a bloodbath, just like a *corrida* [bullfight]. The bull will be Kasparov and the matador Karpov."

Kasparov-Karpov
English Opening

| 1 | c4 | 03 |

Already a minor surprise. Kasparov has nearly always played 1 d4 against Karpov, with a small sprinkling of 1 e4.

| 1 | ... | ♘f6 | 06 |
| 2 | ♘c3 | 03 | e5 | 07 |

Karpov elects to enter a full-blooded English. Perhaps after 2 ... e6 (heading for a Queen's

Gambit) he feared improvements in the complex line 3 e4, which Korchnoi had used to beat Karpov in game 29 of their 1978 match.

| 3 | ♘f3 | 03 | ♘c6 | 07 |
| 4 | g3 | 03 | ♗b4 | 08 |

This variation arises for the first time in a Kasparov-Karpov game. One has to admire the way these two great rivals, after more than a century of games against each other, are still able to extend the frontiers of their conflict.

19

5	♗g2	03	0-0	09
6	0-0	03	e4	15
7	♘g5	04		

Korchnoi-Karpov, match (9) 1974, went 7 ♘e1 ♗xc3 8 dc h6 9 ♘c2.

7	...		♗xc3	16
8	bc	04	♖e8	17
9	f3	04		

The most aggressive continuation, trying to prise open the f-file for attacking purposes. In contrast 9 d3 ed 10 ed h6 11 ♘e4 b6 is considered harmless by theory.

| 9 | ... | | e3!? | 20 |

An alarming innovation which became the main talking point among assembled journalists and grandmasters in Seville for the first two weeks of the championship. Is the move sound . . . why had Kasparov not been prepared for it . . . why did Karpov avoid it when given a second chance in game 4? These were the questions that continued to perplex the experts. Kasparov now pondered for an astonishingly impractical eighty minutes, more than half his allotted time for the whole game, on one single move! With modern time limits (40 moves in 2½ hours) such feats can catapult one into the record books, but are also likely to lead to loss by clock forfeit, or at best to some very bad decisions in the inevitable time scramble.

| 10 | d3 | 84 | | |

10 de is possible. After 10 .. b6 11 e4 ♗b7 followed by ... d6 and ... h6, White's structure is unwieldy and full of weaknesses, but there is some latent dynamism with the thrusts c5 and e5. Curiously, Botvinnik faced a similar situation against Smyslov in 1964, where Kasparov's mentor also chose to meet ... e3 with d3. It is a well-known game and Kasparov should probably have been aware of it. That game went: 1 c4 ♘f6 2 ♘c3 e5 3 g3 ♗b4 4 ♗g2 0-0 5 a3 ♗xc3 6 bc e4 7 ♘h3 ♖e8 8 0-0 d6 9 ♘f4 b6 10 f3 e3 11 d3 ♗b7 12 ♕e1 ♘bd7 13 g4 h6 14 h4 ♘f8 15 ♕g3. Botvinnik eventually won, but mistrusted his opening. His conclusion was that it is too risky for White to leave Black's pawn at e3. Kasparov's preparation, in an opening he hardly ever plays, was found wanting.

| 10 | ... | | d5 | 22 |

Black must circumvent ♘e4, which would cut off his far-flung detachment on e3.

11 ♕b3!? *86*

An artificial-looking move that places the white queen offside. Nevertheless, it may be best. In Seville controversy raged for days over the more natural alternative 11 cd, trying to wrench open the position for White's bishop pair. One line of argument ran 11 cd ♘xd5 12 ♘e4 f5 13 ♕b3 (13 c4? ♘de7! 14 ♘c3 f4! followed by ... ♘f5 favours Black, according to bulletin editor Tamas Georgadze) 13 ... ♘a5 14 ♕a3 fe 15 fe ♘c4! (proposed by Dlugy) 16 dc ♘b6. Here it would appear that White can do nothing, since his pawns are so wretchedly scattered. However, 17 ♕c5 ♗e6 18 ♖b1! keeps White on top, inasmuch as 18 ... ♗xc4 19 ♖xb6 ♗xe2 20 ♖b4 ♗xf1 21 ♗xf1 leaves Black with inadequate compensation. Alternatively, 18 ... ♘xc4 19 ♖xb7 ♘d2 20 ♖e1 followed by ♕xe3. 18 ... ♕c8 may be best, although it allows 19 e5

freeing White's king's bishop and retaining some initiative. So, back to the drawing board. A different branch of the discussion follows on 11 cd ♘xd5 12 ♘e4 f5 13 ♕b3 ♗e6 14 ♘c5 ♗f7! offering a pawn sacrifice. 15 ♘xb7 ♕f6 16 ♗b2 is highly unclear, e.g. 16 ... ♖ab8 17 c4 ♘d4 18 ♗xd4 ♕xd4 19 f4.

Did Karpov reject 9 ... e3 in game 4 because of 10 de? Was he afraid of such hideous complications, or was it because of something later in game 2? This is a riddle that may still be answered at a later stage of the match.

| 11 | ... | ♘a5 | *41* |
| 12 | ♕a3 | *88* | |

An unusual observation post for the queen.

12	...	c6	*54*
13	cd	*89*	cd	*55*
14	f4	*90*	♘c6	*76*

Recentralising the knight before White has time to play ♘f3-d4. The immediate 14 ... ♗g4 also deserves serious attention.

| 15 | ♖b1 | *98* | | |

It may seem strange to play ♖b1 and then block in the rook next move with ♗b2. Kasparov's idea, however, is to hold up Black's ideal formation of ... ♗g4 plus ... ♕d7. Also, in distant complications, the latent power of the rook on the b-file may become useful.

| 15 | ... | ♕c7 | *78* |
| 16 | ♗b2 | *114* | ♗g4 | *96* |

Threatening to destroy White's position by capturing on e2. Kasparov's next move is an impetuous attempt to blast the position open by brute force and wrestle man-to-man with Karpov's king. IM Jon Tisdall, the Reuters correspondent in Seville, came up with an imaginative positional option, namely 17 ♘f3 ♖ad8 18 ♖bc1 ♕c8 19 c4 d4 20 c5 planning ♖c4 to round up Black's d4 pawn. For example, 20 ... ♗h3 21 ♖c4 ♗xg2 22 ♔xg2 ♕g4 23 ♗xd4 ♘xd4 24 ♖xd4 and Black cannot penetrate with his queen to e2. 23 ... ♖xd4 is also met by 24 ♖xd4. Nevertheless, Black has a fine continuation in 20 ... ♗xf3! 21 ♗xf3 h5. White's queen's bishop is then permanently blocked out of combat, while Black has a free hand to develop a kingside initiative with ... h4.

20 ... ♗xf3! is paradoxical, in that it gives up an apparently strong black piece and simultaneously enhances the value of White's

fianchettoed king's bishop, but the exchange is extraordinarily effective.

17 c4   115

Kasparov later said that this was premature and that he could have obtained a clear strategic plus with the manoeuvre 17 ♘f3 ♖ad8 18 ♗a1 followed by ♖b5 and only then c4 breaking open the centre.

17 ...   dc   108

Accepting the challenge. If 17 ... ♗xe2 18 ♖fe1 and cd, while 17 ... d4 18 ♗d5! avoids transposition to the unpleasantly passive line given in the last note but one. 18 ... ♗h5 19 ♘f3 ♖ad8 20 ♗xc6 ♕xc6 21 ♘xd4 ♖xd4 22 ♗xd4 ♗xe2 23 ♕c5 ♗xd3 24 ♕xc6 bc is drawish.

18 ♗xf6   125

Shattering the black king's fortifications, but also throwing most of his centre to the winds. By this stage, though, there was no choice.

18 ...   gf   114
19 ♘e4   125   ♔g7   125

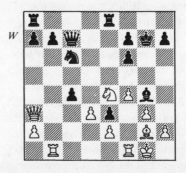

20 dc?   134

Or 20 ♕c3 ♕d8! (20 ... ♖e6? 21 ♘c5! or 20 ... ♕e7 21 ♖xb7!) 21 ♖xb7 ♘d4 22 ♕xc4 ♗e6 23 ♕a4 ♘xe2+ 24 ♔h1 ♕xd3 25 ♘c5 ♘c3! 26 ♕c6 ♕xf1+ 27 ♗xf1 ♗d5+ and Black wins, a variation pointed out by the ingenious Max Dlugy.

However, this moment is the hidden crisis of the game. For over a week it was thought that White had been steaming down the Titanic trail, until former Spanish champion Ernesto Palacios pointed out a staggering possibility here: 20 h3! ♗xe2 21 ♘xf6!! and now:

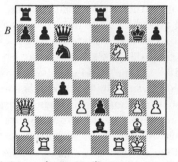

a) **21 ... ♗xf1** 22 ♕c3 with terrible threats to Black's king on the a1-h8 diagonal.

b) **21 ... ♔xf6** 22 ♕b2+ c3 23 ♕xc3+ ♔e7 24 ♖fe1, again with a terrible attack. If 24 ... ♗h5 25 ♕c5+ wins back the bishop.

c) **21 ... ♖ed8!** (the main line) 22 ♕c3 ♘d4 and now the quiet 23 ♖fe1 threatening ♘e8+ deserves attention (not, however, 23 ♖xb7 ♗xf1 and ... ♘e2+). A more forcing line is 23 ♘d5 ♖xd5 (23 ... ♕c5 24 ♖b5 ♕xb5 25 ♕xd4+ is fearfully dangerous with White's knight still in action) 24 ♗xd5 ♕c5 25 ♖b5! (25 ♖fe1 ♕xd5 26 ♖xe2 ♕e5!! 27 ♔f1 ♕d5 or 27 ♔h1 ♕d5+ 28 ♖g2 ♖e8 gives Black enormous compensation) 25 ... ♕xb5 26 ♕xd4+ ♔g8 27 ♗xc4 ♕h5. It is still a complex position, but the likelihood is that one side will deliver a draw by perpetual check, e.g 28 ♖e1 ♕f3 29 ♖xe2 ♕xe2 30 ♗xf7+, followed by many queen checks.

Kasparov himself claimed that 20 ♕c5 would have been very dangerous for Black, although ultimately a draw.

20 ...   ♖ad8 *127*

Karpov brings his final piece into play and White's position becomes well and truly desperate. He has weaknesses everywhere and his pieces are scattered. What ensues is a typical rout after an abortive cavalier attack.

21   ♖b3 *140*

The next day 78-year-old Miguel Najdorf came bouncing into the press room with an intriguing analysis of 21 ♘c3. After 21 ... ♘d4 White has two alternatives. The first, 22 ♗d5 ♖xd5 23 ♘xd5 ♘xe2+ 24 ♔h1 ♕xc4 is very good for Black. Najdorf then produced the following variation after the other move, 22 ♘d5: 22 ... ♕xc4 23 ♘xe3 ♕c3! 24 ♕xc3 ♘xe2+ 25

23

♔h1 ♘xc3 26 ♘xg4 ♘xb1 27
♖xb1 ♖e2 28 ♔g1, but 28 ... h5
29 ♘f2 ♖dd2 is extremely strong.
Another possibility is 21 ... ♖d2
22 ♘d5 ♕a5 23 ♕d6.

| 21 | ... | ♘d4 | 140 |
| 22 | ♖xe3 | 142 | ♕xc4 | 140 |

Kasparov had eight minutes left
to reach the time control at move
40, Karpov ten. More important,
though, Black's counteroffensive
assumes decisive proportions. Here
even 22 ... ♘c2 23 ♕c3 ♘xe3 24
♘xf6 ♔g6 works, according to
Georgadze. But why take unneces-
sary risks?

| 23 | ♔h1 | 142 |

A final try, suggested by Tisdall,
is 23 ♕xa7 protecting along the
a7-g1 diagonal and threatening
♕b6. But after 23 ... ♖e6! 24 h3
♗xe2 25 ♖b1 Black has 25 ... ♗d3,
while 24 ♕xb7 fails to 24 ... f5 25
♘g5 ♖xe3, protecting f7.

23	...	♘f5	146
24	♖d3	144	♗xe2	146
25	♖xd8	144	♖xd8	146

| 26 | ♖e1 | 149 |

Incredibly, Kasparov forgot to
press his clock for two minutes
and forty seconds, thus almost
losing on time. Spanish IM Ricardo
Calvo suggested that this may have
been a Freudian attempt to push
Karpov into time-past, i.e. ever
more firmly into his role of ex-
champion. Perhaps. Others ascribe
it to excessive cogitation over the
10th move having upset Kasparov's
rhythm of thought. A more simple
explanation is the shock of realising
there was no defence.

| 26 | ... | ♖e8 | 146 |
| 27 | ♕a5 | 149 |

27 ♘d6 loses elegantly after 27
... ♘xd6 28 ♕xd6 ♗f3! 29 ♖b1
♕e2 30 ♗xf3 ♕xf3+ and 31 ...
♖e2. After 29 ♕d2 ♖xe1+ 30
♕xe1 ♗xg2+ and 31 ... ♕xa2+
Black is two pawns up in an easily
winning endgame.

| 27 | ... | b5 | 146 |

27 ... ♖xe4 28 ♕xf5 ♗f3 29 ♖g1
♕d3 30 ♕h3 ♖e2 is even more

24

incisive. The last few moves were played in a terrible time scramble.

28	♘d2	149	♕d3	146
29	♘b3	149	♗f3	147
30	♗xf3	149		

Or 30 ♖xe8 ♕f1 mate.

30	...		♕xf3+	147
31	♔g1	149	♖xe1+	147
32	♕xe1	149	♘e3	147

White Resigns

Kasparov	½ 0		½
Karpov	½ 1		1½

GAME THREE, 16 October

After his startling memory lapse during the crisis of the preceding game, it was widely predicted that Kasparov would take a time-out and use the weekend to recover his balance.

But noting that Karpov had lost on time in the eighth game in London, Bleys Rose, a chess expert from Connecticut writing for the US magazine *Chess Life*, said Kasparov's best bet was to come back as soon as possible. "He's got to show Karpov that it isn't such a big deal, that he hasn't suffered a deadly blow."

Kasparov obviously shared this view. He turned up on Friday and held an easy draw with Black after improving on game 1. The champion was back on his feet.

Karpov-Kasparov
Neo Grünfeld Defence

1	d4	00	♘f6	00
2	c4	00	g6	00
3	g3	00		

Once again, Karpov shows that he is not yet ready to join a serious battle in the Grünfeld main lines.

3	...		c6	00
4	♗g2	00	d5	00
5	cd	00	cd	00
6	♘f3	00	♗g7	00
7	♘c3	00	0-0	00
8	♘e5	00	e6	00
9	0-0	00	♘fd7	00
10	f4	04	♘c6	12
11	♗e3	05	♘b6	15
12	♗f2	05		

So far, an exact duplication of game 1, where we claimed that White could have seized a middle-game advantage by playing the sharp advance g4 at a later stage. Kasparov seems to agree that White could have gained the advantage in that earlier game, since he now introduces a novelty, replacing his original choice 12 ... ♗d7.

12	...		♘e7	15
13	a4	11	a5	18
14	♕b3	15		

Karpov proceeds to concentrate his entire army against Black's queen's wing. His main hope must be to penetrate down the c-file or inflict a weakness there, such as a backward pawn on c6.

26

14	...		&d7	21
15	&fc1	21	&c6	28
16	&b5	22	&bc8	58

A splendid solution to Black's difficulties, which cuts the Gordian knot of White's pressure. Other, perhaps less convincing, possibilities are 16 ... &b8 or the speculative pawn sacrifice 16 ... &f5!? 17 &xc6 bc 18 &xc6 &c4 19 e4 &d2 20 &d3 &xe4 21 &xe4 de 22 &xe4, when Black's compensation is inadequate.

17 e3?! 44

This move is too slow. Perhaps Karpov had overlooked Black's defensive trick coming in reply to 19 &xc6. If White can claim any advantage it must be by 17 &c2, planning the immediate doubling of rooks on the c-file.

| 17 | ... | | &d6 | 71 |
| 18 | &xd6 | 52 | &xd6 | 71 |

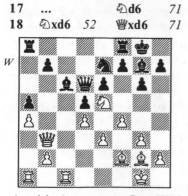

A critical moment. Can White play 19 &xc6? It is clear that 19 ...

&xc6 20 &xb7 &b4 21 &b5 gives Black very little for his pawn. The answer is 19 ... bc! 20 &c5 (others are too slow) 20 ... &fb8 21 &c2 &xb2! 22 &xb2 &xc5 23 &b7 &a7 and Black comes out on top.

19	&e1	59	&fb8	75
20	&f1	88	f6	90
21	&f3	88		

Here 21 &xc6 &xc6 is evidently fine for Black, who would control all of the queenside dark squares.

21	...		&d7	90
22	&c2	98	&f5	93
23	&d2	99	&d6	94
24	b3	99	&c8	105

The strategic pendulum has swung somewhat in Black's favour. He enjoys the dual advantage of more flexible central pawns and a White weakness on e4. The best way of utilising both trumps would be 24 ... &e8 25 &d3 (for example) 25 ... &f7 26 e4 (before Black plays ... e5) 26 ... de 27 &xe4 &d5 and Black has a slight edge. Kasparov's plan is less effective.

25	&d1	100	h6	109
26	&e1	107	g5	110
27	&a2	108	&e8	126
28	&ac2	110	&f8	135
29	&d3	117	g4	139

Draw Agreed

Black had only eleven minutes left, and 30 &d2 is safe enough.

| Kasparov | ½ 0 ½ | 1 |
| Karpov | ½ 1 ½ | 2 |

GAME FOUR, 19 October

After the weekend break Kasparov was indeed back on his best form for this, their 100th championship game. He built up a dangerous kingside initiative with the white pieces, forcing Karpov to transpose into an ending and cede a pawn. When Karpov missed the best defence at the end of a mutual time scramble, Kasparov adjourned two pawns up.

General expectation the following morning that Karpov would resign without resumption led, at one point, to confusion in the press room. Just before noon a match official announced to reporters that Karpov had in fact resigned. However, when chief arbiter Gijssen arrived at the Lope de Vega theatre he said he had heard nothing about it. On telephoning Karpov's villa, he was informed that rumours of Karpov's resignation were premature. But two hours later Gijssen reappeared to announce that – this time – Karpov had definitely resigned.

At the start of the game itself Karpov had arrived four minutes late and Kasparov sportingly allowed his own clock to run until the challenger came to the board. The next day Spanish Chess Federation president Roman Toran explained that Karpov's driver had arrived late at the villa to take him to the game.

A rather deeper mystery, still unresolved, was Karpov's declining to repeat his stunning 9 ... e3 innovation from game 2. Prepared by Karpov before his 1981 encounter with Korchnoi in Merano, it had served him extraordinarily well. Perhaps he feared that the Kasparov camp, after four days to think about it, might have come up with an answer.

"It was a fine technical win," commented Leontxo Garcia, *El Pais* correspondent and co-host of the nightly TV programme on the match, just after Kasparov drew level. "Today Kasparov's characteristic pride and energy have won through over the nerves he was exhibiting earlier."

Kasparov-Karpov
English Opening

1	c4	04	♘f6	00
2	♘c3	04	e5	00
3	♘f3	04	♘c6	00
4	g3	04	♗b4	01
5	♗g2	04	0-0	06
6	0-0	04	e4	06
7	♘g5	04	♗xc3	06
8	bc	04	♖e8	21
9	f3	04	ef	21

One of the mysteries of the universe, as yet unanswered, is why Kasparov allowed 9 ... e3 and why Karpov declined to repeat it. In an interview for the US newspaper *USA Today* Karpov simply stated that he just did not want to repeat such a complicated line. That may well, in fact, be the solution.

10 ♘xf3 04 ♕e7 21

An unusual move and not a particularly impressive one. The normal theoretical line is 10 ... d5 11 cd ♕xd5. Karpov's choice leaves his queen on e7 somewhat exposed to harassment, although this was as yet not easy to perceive.

11 e3 11 ♘e5 24

A novelty, but not one that is likely to gain a great following. Instead 11 ... d6 12 d3 ♗g4 13 h3 ♗d7 14 e4 strongly favours White, as in Smyslov-Peev, Capablanca Memorial 1973.

12 ♘d4 41

A typical pawn offer from Kasparov to increase his transboard dynamism should Black accept. Karpov wisely declines, doubtless because White has so many alluring ways of seizing the initiative, e.g. 12 ... ♘xc4 13 ♘f5 ♕e5 14 d3 ♘xc3 15 ♖b1 ♘d6 (15 ... ♘e5 is more resilient) 16 ♘xg7 ♔xg7 17 ♗b2, a variation given by Georgadze. Another idea in the above line is 14 ♕f3 d5 15 ♘h6+ ♔f8 16 ♕xd5, possible since 16 ... ♘xd5 stumbles into 17 ♖xf7 mate.

In similar vein is 12 ... ♘xc4 13 ♘f5 ♕e5 (or 13 ... ♕c5) 14 d4 ♕a5 15 ♕d3 d5 16 ♘h6+ ♔f8 17 ♕xh7 threatening ♕g8+ and ♖xf6.

In all of these lines White's attack is based on a spectacular breakthrough at the sensitive point f7. It would have been foolhardy to accept the pawn on c4 and unleash Kasparov in this fashion.

12 ... ♘d3 43
13 ♕e2 75

Also dangerous, though less clear-cut than the pawn sacrifice

29

on c4, is 13 ♘f5 ♕c5 14 ♕e2 ♘xc1 15 ♖axc1 d6 16 d4 ♕a5 17 ♘h6+ ♔f8 18 c5 dc 19 ♕h5, when Black of course does not take the queen but parries with 19 ... ♗e6.

This is the kind of violent assault one might expect from Kasparov, but having jettisoned caution to the winds in game 2 he evidently wished to pursue a more sober strategic course in this game. His attitude is justifiable; Karpov's refusal to take the pawn has ceded White an excellent position with no need to incur excessive risks.

13	...	♘xc1	45
14	♖axc1 75	d6	46
15	♖f4	79	

Laying the foundation for a massive attack down the f-file.

15	...	c6	53

The intention is to obstruct the diagonal of White's bishop. 15 ... c5 is an alternative, although Ulf Andersson condemned it after 16 ♘f5 ♗xf5 17 ♖xf5, when White's bishop is paramount.

16	♖cf1 83	♕e5	72

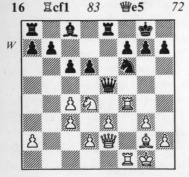

White's advantage is clear and is based on three factors: a central pawn majority, great pressure from the doubled rooks and a highly active bishop directed towards Black's queen's flank.

17	♕d3	97	♗d7	89

17 ... ♕e7 is a more subtle means of defence, saving a tempo after 18 ♘f5 ♗xf5 and leaving the black queen less prone to attack.

18	♘f5	104	♗xf5	92
19	♖xf5	105	♕e6	92
20	♕d4	108		

Gufeld compared the steady, step-by-step approach of the white queen into its attack position to a cat stealthily stealing up on its prey before the pounce.

20	...	♖e7	99

At this point Kasparov must have been tempted by 21 ♖xf6, sacrificing the exchange in order to wipe out Black's king's defences, e.g. 21 ... gf 22 ♖xf6 ♕e5 23 ♕g4+ ♔h8 24 ♖f5 ♕e6 25 ♕f4. This would be reminiscent of a game won by Portisch against Karpov at San Antonio 1972. However, here and two moves later Kasparov sees no need to rush things.

21	♕h4	116	♘d7	124
22	♗h3	119	♘f8	124
23	♖5f3	123		

There are certainly other spectacular continuations available, such as 23 ♖xf7 or 23 ♖b5, but this patient retreat neatly forces a won ending. White exploits the fact that the black queen is tied down to the protection of his rook. In view of this Black's next few moves are obligatory.

23 ♖b5 is in fact worth a closer look. In his comment for *USA Today* Karpov claimed it was the strongest. In the bulletin Georgadze gives the line 23 ... ♘g6 24 ♗xe6 ♘xh4 25 ♖xf7 ♖xe6 26 ♖bxb7 with crushing compensation for the piece. However, a better defence resides in 25 ... ♖xf7 26 ♗xf7+ ♔f8 27 ♖xb7 ♘f3+ 28 ♔g2 ♘xd2 29 ♗e6 ♖e8 30 ♖f7+ ♔g8 and Black is still clinging to life.

Max Dlugy was all for the cavalier 23 ♖g5, but it is no surprise after game 2 that Kasparov prefers one bird in the hand . . .

23	...		♛e5	126
24	d4	123	♛e4	128
25	♛xe4	124	♖xe4	128
26	♖xf7	124	♖xe3	131
27	d5	126		

Crushing, for if 27 ... cd 28 ♗g2 wins at once by gaining deadly access for the bishop to d5. Similarly, 27 ... ♖xc3? loses to 28 ♖xf8+ ♖xf8 29 ♗e6+. In fact there is no good move left.

| 27 | ... | | ♖ae8 | 137 |

Now Kasparov could have terminated the game in a brisk flourish with 28 c5, which wins outright, e.g. 28 ... dc 29 d6 ♖d3 30 ♖xf8+ and ♗e6+ as before. A more stalwart defence is 29 ... ♖d8 30 d7 ♘g6, as proposed by IM William Watson, briefly in Seville en route between tournaments. Nevertheless 31 ♗g4 h6 32 ♔g2, preparing h4 and ♗h5 or ♗f5 if Black moves his king, will prove sufficient.

Instead the world champion makes an incautious capture and has to win the game all over again.

28	♖xb7?	131	cd	137
29	cd	132	♖3e7	138
30	♖fb1	133	h5?	140

A total waste of time. Black has to centralise his king at once with 30 ... ♔f7, when it is extraordinarily hard to demonstrate a clear advantage for White. 31 ♖f1+ ♔g8 simply repeats moves, while with his king on f7 Black threatens to play ... ♖xb7 and ... ♖e7. Exchange of all rooks favours Black's defence as in the pure minor piece ending the white bishop is somewhat restricted by the pawn on d5. Furthermore the black knight has fine squares on c5 and e5.

31

Karpov's move not only weakens his pawns but fails to set up a challenge to White's rooks on the 7th rank.

31 a4 *137*

Planning to push the pawn to a6 where it will represent a constant menace if at least one pair of rooks stays on the board.

Another method is 31 ☖xe7 ☖xe7 32 ☖b8 threatening ♗e6+ and ☖d8. Black will resist with 32 ... g5 33 ☖d8 g4 and ... ☖d7, again threatening the all-important trade of rooks.

31	**...**		**g5**	*142*
32	**♗f5**	*137*	**♔g7**	*142*
33	**a5**	*141*	**♔f6**	*144*
34	**♗d3**	*142*	**☖xb7**	*147*

Not, of course, 34 ... ☖e3? 35 ☖f1+ ♔e5 36 ☖f5 mate.

35	**☖xb7**	*142*	**☖e3**	*147*
36	**♗b5**	*143*	**☖xc3**	*148*
37	**☖xa7**	*144*	**♘g6**	*148*

At last Black activates his knight.

38 ☖d7 *144*

The last chance now is 38 ... ♔e5 resolutely defending the pawn on d6. White still wins but the process is not so simple: 39 ☖g7 ♔f6 40 ☖b7 ♔e5 41 ♗e8 is decisive. If 40 ... ☖a3 41 a6 ♘e5 42 a7 ☖a2 43 h3 (not 43 ♗c6 ♘f3+ 44 ♔f1

♘xh2+ 45 ♔e1 h4 46 gh g4 and suddenly White faces major problems; 43 ... ☖d2 also looks playable but fails to 44 ☖b3) 43 ... ☖d2 44 ♔f1 and dreams of perpetual check evaporate.

38 ... **♘e5** *148*

Here the two-piece attack is even more illusory. White now wins at a canter.

39	**☖xd6+**	*145*	**♔f5**	*148*
40	**a6**	*145*	**☖a3**	*148*
41	**☖d8**	*159*	**Resigns**	

White's 41st was sealed, but as is his wont in manifestly lost positions Karpov did not want to be shown and resigned without resumption. The clearest winning line goes: 41 ... ☖a2 42 ☖f8+ ♔e4 43 d6 ♘f3+ 44 ☖xf3 ♔xf3 45 d7 ☖a1+ 46 ♗f1 ☖d1 47 a7.

Kasparov	½ 0 ½ 1	2
Karpov	½ 1 ½ 0	2

GAME FIVE, 23 October

After his loss Karpov took the first of his time-outs on Wednesday, postponing the fifth game until Friday. It seemed as if Kasparov was back on top of the world, but the next two days were to prove most eventful for the 24-year-old from Baku. By Friday night, an old friend would have left the Politburo, his Schweppes commercial would have been shown throughout Spain, and Karpov would regain the lead after a hideous blunder by Kasparov in a frantic time scramble.

The first news came on Wednesday evening from Moscow – TASS announced that Geidar Aliev had been retired from the Politburo for "reasons of health". Although considered an early supporter of Mikhail Gorbachov, he had risen under the patronage of Leonid Brezhnev, and the industries for which he was responsible had been performing poorly and had even been criticised in the state-run media.

Although the announcement immediately set the tongues wagging in Seville, more thoughtful analyses quickly dismissed any major significance for Kasparov. It is true that Aliev helped Kasparov through some very prickly situations between 1981 and 1983, but as Kasparov makes clear in *Child of Change*, it was Alexander Yakovlev who intervened in 1985 to protect Kasparov when, as the latter claims, Soviet sports officials tried to have him banned for speaking out. Yakovlev, now a full-time Politburo member, is one of Gorbachov's closest advisers. Moreover it was already known around the time of the Dubai olympiad that Aliev's position was becoming increasingly weak.

The Kremlinology was put strictly on hold by Thursday night, however, as chessplayers huddled around the nearest TV set for the unveiling of Kasparov's commercial for Schweppes tonic water. This was, as mentioned, the first ever Western TV advertisement to feature a Soviet citizen, and it also contained appearances by a blonde Finnish model and a French actor famous throughout Spain as "Mr Schweppes" for the last nine years.

33

Kasparov is seated at a board when suddenly Mr Schweppes arrives. They recognise each other and exchange greetings. Kasparov opens a bottle of tonic water with a knight he lifts off the chess board. Mr Schweppes tries to copy Kasparov's technique but fails, and Kasparov begins to laugh. As the 20-second segment ends, the drink is described as "Kasparov's Passion".

"We decided to do a TV commercial when we realised what a very good actor he was," commented John de Zulueta, the marketing director for Schweppes in Spain. "At first we wanted to use a very serious type of story, but we changed it when we saw that Gary had such an effervescent type of personality," he added. The deal was struck by Andrew Page, Kasparov's British manager. A storyboard of the commercial had been sent to the Soviet sports committee for their prior approval.

In the following day's game Kasparov once again replied with his favourite Grünfeld Defence. Karpov countered with an unusual move in the Exchange Variation, winning a pawn but allowing Kasparov's pieces to become dangerously active. In an increasingly tense battle Kasparov used more and more of his time, already eaten into by a 64-minute think on move 14. First, Kasparov missed a probable chance of advantage on move 25, then a series of draws. Suddenly he cracked with a final terrible blunder. At one moment the automatic time-counter on the video screens moved to 2.30. With his king stripped of defences, a rook en prise and no time, Kasparov resigned.

The reaction was harsh, if predictable. Danish international master Bjarke Kristensen commented: "It was brainless. Kasparov had a good position, there was no need to get into such time trouble."

So game 4 was wiped clean off the slate. Karpov's brinkmanship had regained him the lead. Boris Spassky was gone from Seville, but his words were not forgotten. As Max Dlugy said, "Kasparov seemed sure he was going to win. He started to play like he couldn't possibly lose, and that killed him."

Karpov-Kasparov
Grünfeld Defence

1	d4	♘f6
2	c4	g6
3	♘c3	d5
4	cd	

For the first time in this match Karpov chooses 'the man's move' against the Grünfeld. The Exchange Variation was the line employed twice by Spassky to beat Fischer, at Santa Monica 1966 and Siegen 1970. Significantly, Fischer utterly renounced the Grünfeld in his 1972 title challenge against Spassky.

4	...		♘xd5	
5	e4		♘xc3	
6	bc		♗g7	
7	♗c4		c5	
8	♘e2	04	♘c6	03
9	♗e3		0-0	
10	0-0		♗g4	
11	f3		♘a5	04

Slightly unusual, though it will normally result in simple transposition to the main line, which is 11 ... cd.

| 12 | ♗xf7+ | 05 | | |

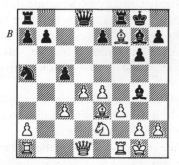

But this is hardly ever played. White gains a virtually worthless doubled pawn and cedes Black some initiative. Nonetheless, against Kasparov it may well be a finely chosen psychological ploy. Karpov and his team of seconds must have appreciated after so many games that Kasparov does not feel comfortable when his own king is somewhat exposed. This rare move rips away some of the protection around the black king and forces Kasparov into some difficult thinking at the board. White's extra pawn may look feeble now, but in later play the trio of kingside pawns lends his king greater security than Kasparov's.

12	...		♖xf7	04
13	fg	05	♖xf1+	08
14	♔xf1	05	♕d6	72

Karpov's cunning already pays off. Black's position is now fully playable (indeed Kasparov was to repeat it in subsequent games) but Kasparov had used up one hour and five minutes over this single move – that amounts to almost half of his entire allotted time for the first session of play.

Note that Black avoids 14 ... cd, doubtless fearing 15 ♗xd4 in reply. 15 cd would just transpose to older lines where Black is meant to have easy equality.

In the further course of this game (and in game 7 to come) there is a fascinating constant tension as to when or whether Black should play ... cd or White dc.

| 15 | e5 | 16 | | |

An intriguing decision and certainly correct.

Twenty years ago this would have been condemned as positional and strategic capitulation, since White irrevocably weakens his

35

light squares and hems in his own bishop. Nowadays, partly as a result of games by Karpov himself, there is a deeper appreciation of such situations. White's pawn wedge in the centre still has to be dismantled, and while it clings to life it presents a mighty obstacle to Black's bishop on g7. In addition, White may flick in the move g5 to deprive the black bishop of its other escape route. That possibility does not materialise here but it plays a role in game 7. Finally, if Black does work hard to regain his pawn there is still a danger that White may emerge into an endgame with a minor plus, such as control of the b-file.

All in all, this is a colossally fascinating variation and a major contribution from this match to the modern theory of openings.

| 15 | ... | | ♕d5 | 81 |
| 16 | ♗f2 | 26 | ♖f8 | 93 |

The most natural move, though Kasparov abandoned it in game 7,

preferring 16 ... ♖d8. Quite why is not clear, since Black obtains a fine position in this game.

17 ♔g1   30

Played quickly, yet after this the black bishop leaps into action. If there is a refutation of 16 ... ♖f8 it should be at this stage, but it is not easy to detect. 17 ♘g1 planning ♘f3 is pointless after 17 ... ♕c4+. The other main possibility is 17 g5, but 17 ... ♕e4 18 ♔g1 ♕f5 19 ♕e1 ♕xg5 20 ♘g3 cd 21 cd ♘c4 leaves Black with very few problems to solve. In other lines White gets into trouble if he tries too hard to retain the extra pawn, e.g. 19 ♗e3 ♘c4 20 ♕b3 ♕d3.

Perhaps the most promising for White is 17 g5 ♕e4 18 ♘g1 ♘c4 19 ♘f3 ♘e3+ 20 ♗xe3 ♕xe3 21 ♕b3+ ♔h8 22 ♖e1 ♕xg5 23 ♕xb7. Even here White is sacrificing his king safety for a small material plus. So we have another of the theoretical puzzles of this match: 16 ... ♖f8 looks no worse than 16 ... ♖d8, yet it was not repeated in the next game where Kasparov was Black.

17 ...   ♗h6   96

Freedom at last.

18 h4   48

Trying to crowd the black bishop out of play, but Kasparov finds a way to fling it forwards into White's vital areas. A subsidiary point of 18 h4 is to use the white pawns to batter against Black's slightly depleted king's flank.

18	...		♕f7	98
19	♗g3	49	♗e3+	99
20	♔h2	49	♕c4	115

Kasparov's position is excellent – well worth a pawn's investment – but just compare the relative clock times. Remember, there are 150 minutes available to each player to reach the first time control at move 40. Kasparov had already consumed more than twice as much time as Karpov.

| 21 | ♖b1 | 81 | | |

At last Karpov starts to think. This move is the beginning of a reorganising manoeuvre. In the bulletin Georgadze states that 21 d5 ♕xg4 22 d6 e6 favours Black.

| 21 | ... | | b6 | 121 |
| 22 | ♖b2!? | 85 | | |

Here White should have considered 22 dc ♗xc5 23 ♘d4, which is very complicated but can lead to a balanced endgame after 23 ... ♕xa2 24 h5 ♘c4 25 hg ♘e3 26 ♕b3+ ♕xb3 27 ♘xb3 ♘xg4+. Here, and subsequently, Karpov plays to increase the tension, clearly hoping to capitalise on Black's time shortage.

22	...		♕d5	130
23	♕d3	87	♘c4	131
24	♖b1	87	b5!	132

Karpov could now have invited a draw by 25 ♖xb5 ♘xe5 26 ♖xc5 (26 ♗xe5 ♖f2 wins) 26 ... ♘xg4+ 27 ♔h3 ♕d7, when Black probably

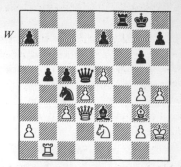

has nothing better than perpetual check. But 27 ... ♘d2 is awkward for White, e.g. a) 26 ♖xc5 ♕e6 and the threat of ... ♕xg4 combined with ... ♘f1+ is hard to parry. After 27 ♔h1 ♖f1+ 28 ♔h2 Black can either repeat or try for more; b) 26 ♔h3 ♖f1 27 ♔h2 (27 ♕xe3 ♖h1+ 28 ♗h2 ♖xh2+!) 27 ... ♘f3+! winning.

| 25 | ♔h3 | 104 | a6? | 133 |

Precisely the wrong moment to be timid. Black should have struck out at once against the base of White's pawn chain with 25 ... b4, after which it is difficult to find a truly satisfactory continuation for White. For example, 25 ... b4 26 cb cd. Black is still a pawn down, but his passed d-pawn is very powerful and there are various promising lines such as 27 ♕b3 (to pin Black's knight) 27 ... d3 or 27 ... h5.

Kasparov stated after the game that 25 ... b4 would have given him the advantage.

| 26 | ♘g1 | 108 | | |

Karpov admits that he cannot hold his centre, but as the extra pawn vanishes and the board bursts into flames, it is Karpov who holds the whip hand in terms of substantial extra time on the clock.

26	...		cd	144
27	♘f3	131	♖d8	145
28	a4	132		

Clearing away weaknesses and opening lines for the time scramble. Not, however, 28 cd ♗xd4 29 ♖d1? ♘b2 winning material.

| 28 | ... | | dc | 145 |
| 29 | ♕xc3 | 132 | ♕e6 | 146 |

Kasparov boldly continues to complicate matters in his own time trouble. After the simple 29 ... ♕d3 30 ♕xd3 ♖xd3 31 ab ♘a3 it is difficult to conceive that Black can lose. Kasparov resolves to hazard all on one wild gamble to strike at the cornered white king. Perhaps he was deluded by memories of a similar triumph in the decisive game 22 of the last match. His problem here is that the white king is not cornered enough.

| 30 | ♔h2 | 134 | ba | 147 |
| 31 | ♖b4 | 135 | ♘d2 | 147 |

The bishop is of course immune since it has the ... ♘f1+ lifeline.

| 32 | ♖xa4 | 135 | ♘f1+ | 148 |

Going for broke with only two minutes on his clock for the next eight moves.

Naturally, 32 ... ♘xf3+ 33 gf ♗d2 leads to a dead even position.

| 33 | ♔h3 | 135 | ♖d1 | 149 |

Another barbaric move. With his clock flag hanging, poised to drop and forfeit him on time, an ordinary mortal would have kept his forces together for safety's sake, instead of hurling them like this into the opponent's entrails.

| 34 | ♕c2 | 142 | | |

Planning to win on time, otherwise he would have chosen the objectively best 34 ♖xa6 ♕xa6 35 ♕b3+ winning a good pawn.

| 34 | ... | | ♖c1 | 149 |
| 35 | ♕e2 | 142 | | |

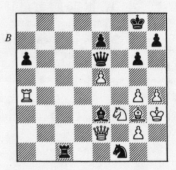

The crisis of the game is reached. Kasparov now tries to give mate by nailing the white king on h3. After the game the fantastic possibility 35 ... g5 was mentioned to us by a very authoritative source, but it is hard to believe that such a shot can hold up.

| 35 | ... | | h5 | 149 |
| 36 | ♗e1 | 142 | ♕d7?? | 149 |

Kasparov misses his last chance to hold the draw, which he could do with the spectacular 36 ... ♖a1 exploiting the fact that White's rook is tied to the defence of the pawn on g4. White's sole reply is 37 ♕c4, when 37 ... ♕xc4 38 ♖xc4 ♔f7 is tenable. White must avoid the trap 37 ♕c2? ♗f4 38 ♖xf4 hg+ 39 ♖xg4 ♕xg4+ 40 ♔xg4 ♘e3+ forking king and queen.

37   ♕xa6 *142* **♖a1** *149*

One move too late. Kasparov, in the desperate rush to complete his moves, overlooks that the all-important g6 pawn is not protected.

38   ♕xg6+ *142* **Resigns**

Absolute demolition. A tragedy for Kasparov who certainly did not need to lose this game.

| Kasparov | ½ | 0 | ½ | 1 | 0 | | 2 |
| Karpov | ½ | 1 | ½ | 0 | 1 | | 3 |

GAME SIX, 26 October

At the end of the fifth game the players left the Lope de Vega theatre in rather different spirits: Karpov delighted with his second victory in only five games; Kasparov with wasted opportunities flashing before his eyes.

Dejected after his self-immolation in the previous game, Kasparov took no risks at all in today's game, preferring to maintain a very small edge and eliminate any possibility of losing.

Indeed the sixth game was a quiet affair, a kind of Closed Sicilian with colours reversed where Kasparov missed his best continuation at move 16. When they agreed a draw at move 28 White's initiative had been completely neutralised.

An easy draw with the black pieces and Karpov retains his lead. Morale was clearly high in Karpov's camp and among his closest supporters. But what about Natasha, the most watched member of Karpov's delegation, always in the audience at the start of play and frequently in the hall?

One answer came from the official match bulletin on game 6. It ran a front page piece about the new Mrs Karpov, translated, along with annotations by GM Tamas Georgadze and features of general interest, into English. The quaintly worded article concluded as follows:

"Smiling when she encounters the glance of sympathetic eyes, tense and serious when she loses herself in the technical depths of the monitors, Natalya personifies the help which doesn't get its chance, the removed support which longs to lend itself and never manages to the powerless struggle. However, she stays there, evening upon evening, full of attention, smiling, serious, like a chilly iceberg not scared by anything, while inside there hide the flames of desire for a victory she has been dreaming of."

Kasparov-Karpov
English Opening

1	c4		e5	
2	♘c3		♘c6	
3	g3		g6	

It is hard to say which of the players truly diverges first from the play in games 2 and 4. Kasparov could, for example, have tried 3 ♘f3 inviting ... ♘f6, while Karpov could have parried 3 g3 with 3 ... ♘f6 for his part, inviting 4 ♗g2 ♗b4 5 ♘f3 etc, transposing into the lines we saw in Kasparov's first two games with White. Perhaps both players just wanted a respite from the analytical rigours of the English Four Knights as used in those earlier encounters.

4	♗g2	01	d6	04
5	♖b1	15	♗f5	07

A strange idea. It would seem somewhat naive to attack White's rook in this forthright fashion, but the move is hard to refute.

6	d3	17	♕d7	
7	b4	19		

Consistent strategy, pushing forward on the queenside. Kasparov had suffered against Ljubojević playing the Black side of a similar opening in one of his two losses at the world blitz in Brussels earlier in the year, so perhaps he was impressed by Ljubo's treatment . . .

7	...		♗g7	10
8	b5	24	♘d8	10

9	♘d5	25		

This great leap forwards loses tempi but virtually obliges Black to loosen his pawn structure.

9	...		c6	20

Best. There are all sorts of traps lurking if Black is unwary, e.g. 9 ... ♘f6 10 ♗h6 ♘xd5 11 ♗xg7 ♘c3 12 ♕b3 ♖g8 13 ♕xc3 ♖xg7, when Black is seriously disorganised.

10	bc	26	bc	21
11	♘c3	38		

11 ♘e3 ♗e6 12 ♘f3 is also worth a thought (in fact, twelve minutes' worth).

11	...		♘e7	44
12	♗a3	42	0-0	
13	♘f3	48	h6	
14	0-0		♗e6	51
15	♕a4	54	f5	52

In spite of, or indeed because of, the peregrinations of the white knight, Kasparov has a fine position. Active play on the queenside, control of the b-file and long-range bishops eyeing Black's pawns on d6 and c6 – all this should amount

41

to something.

After the game Kasparov was reputedly angry that he had failed to make more of his advantage, but the only real improvement the press room grandmasters could unearth was 16 ♖b3, expeditiously doubling rooks on the open b-file. Another plus to 16 ♖b3 is that it adds lateral protection to the c3 knight against sudden tactical incursions such as ... e4. White's choice in the game is excessively dilatory.

16	♘d2	54	♘f7	74
17	♖b3	77	♖ab8	75
18	♖fb1	78	♖xb3	75
19	♖xb3	79	♖c8	77
20	♕a6	82	♘d8	82

Karpov adroitly plugs all the holes and possible ports of entry in his queen's wing.

21	♗b4	101	♖b8	88

22	♘a4	102		

Or 22 ♗a5 ♖xb3 23 ♘xb3 ♕b7 24 ♕xb7 ♘xb7 25 ♗c7 e4 with equality according to Georgadze in the bulletin.

22	...		♔f7	91
23	♗c3	109	♖xb3	102
24	ab	109		

The last slim chance, perhaps, is 24 ♘xb3, but investigations revealed nothing tangible for White.

24	...		♕c7	106
25	e3	111	♗c8	120
26	♕a5			

White evidently cannot avoid the trade of queens.

26	...		♕xa5	120
27	♗xa5	112	♘e6	120
28	♗b4			

In playing this Kasparov offered a draw, which Karpov immediately accepted.

Draw Agreed

Kasparov	½ 0 ½ 1 0 ½	2½
Karpov	½ 1 ½ 0 1 ½	3½

GAME SEVEN, 30 October

After a two-day rest following Kasparov's first time out, the seventh game was the most closely contested of the match so far.

Continuing their duel in the Grünfeld, Kasparov produced a new idea on move 16. Faced with a brilliant Karpovian manoeuvre which switched the white queen into the attack, Kasparov missed several of his best alternatives. Karpov piled on the pressure as his opponent struggled in time trouble, and the game was adjourned in an ending where Black, the exchange for two pawns down, would have to tread extremely carefully to draw.

If there was nothing unusual so far, the second session was remarkable indeed. When play resumed Karpov quickly swapped off the queens, leaving Black with seemingly little option but to set up a "fortress" defence. Kasparov, however, broke out with a series of pawn advances which appeared to create all kinds of textbook weaknesses.

"Never in my life did I see such bad endgame play," exclaimed Miguel Najdorf, echoing the views of the grandmaster analysis table. Nearby, Soviet analysts were heard muttering "Ujarsni!" ("Terrible!") to describe Kasparov's strategy.

But members of Kasparov's delegation in the press room (not his seconds) were acting mysteriously. They appeared quite calm and carefree as they watched the video screens.

Karpov sank deeper and deeper into thought. Suddenly both players flashed out their moves and White began to eat up the black pawns. Three of Kasparov's pawns fell, but the sole survivor remained with a clear run to the queening square. Kasparov won the resulting promotion race by one tempo, reaching a well-known drawn queen and pawn ending.

As the crowd rewarded both players with an ovation, Seyavush Yeganov, Kasparov's head of delegation, claimed it had all been analysis. He himself had seen the 77th move position – an amazing 35 moves after resumption – on a board at Kasparov's villa that morning.

Even though Karpov retained his lead and Kasparov had walked a tightrope for most of the game, the 24-year-old champion appeared jubilant. Not only had Karpov fallen an hour behind on the clock in the second session, Kasparov's seconds had completely out-analysed the Karpov team.

After chatting with Kasparov on Sunday, Najdorf sensed the title-holder's new-found confidence. "He's feeling good. I think he is going to win the 8th game," Najdorf concluded.

Karpov-Kasparov
Grünfeld Defence

1	d4	00	♘f6	00
2	c4	00	g6	00
3	♘c3	00	d5	01

Kasparov continues to show a touching faith in the Grünfeld Defence, even though his record against Karpov with it is now perhaps even worse than with the Orthodox Defence to the Queen's Gambit. Game 7 of the match here in Seville was the thirteenth outing for Kasparov's Grünfeld. Thirteen is Kasparov's lucky number. He was born on 13 April, he is the thirteenth world champion, etc. We are still not sure after the confusing events of game 7 whether thirteen was propitious or otherwise for him in this case.

4	cd	02	♘xd5	01
5	e4	02	♘xc3	01
6	bc	02	♗g7	01
7	♗c4	02	c5	01
8	♘e2	03	♘c6	02
9	♗e3	04	0-0	02
10	0-0	04	♗g4	02

11	f3	05	♘a5	02
12	♗xf7+	06		

Karpov had introduced this variation in game 5 and won, although his position was not that convincing at most stages. It had the inestimable advantage, however, of making Kasparov think. In fact, Karpov has reverted here to the method on which he built his reputation against Korchnoi – fast moves, not necessarily the best, but sufficient to make a deep-thinking opponent run short of time.

12	...		♖xf7	02
13	fg	07	♖xf1+	03
14	♔xf1	07	♕d6	16
15	e5	13	♕d5	21
16	♗f2	13	♖d8	46

44

Kasparov's innovation over game 5. Significantly, the world champion had already used up 46 minutes of the 150 available for the first 40 moves, though he must still have been within the perimeters of his preparation between games 5 and 7.

Black's earlier try had, of course, been 16 ... ♖f8.

17 ♕c1   16

Karpov is the all-time champion of such small moves – so often an insignificant-looking move on his part turns out to be part of a grand design.

17 ...   ♕e4   48

Black's roving queen provokes weaknesses in White's pawn carapace, but White is also encouraged to play g5 locking in Black's bishop.

18	**g5**	*23*	**♕f5**	*65*
19	**h4**	*35*	**♘c4**	*77*
20	**♔g1**	*36*	**♕g4**	*78*
21	**a4!**	*43*		

A brilliant unravelling plan in connection with his next move. White's position appears to have stalled but a4 plus ♖a2 brings it back to life. Kasparov, meanwhile, was already beginning to run significantly behind on time.

21 ...   h6   89

This is the only way to drum up counterplay, but it implies an obvious weakening of his king's field which Karpov quickly exploits.

22 ♖a2   58   hg   102

23   ♕b1   78

With dual threats of ♕b3 pinning the c4 knight and ♕xg6, Kasparov's nemesis in game 5. The champion now used up seventeen precious minutes over his reply, almost as if he had overlooked or underestimated ♕b1. If he had cast his mind back to the award-winning game 11 of the 1986 match, he would have been forewarned of Karpov's mysterious penchant for following up ♕e1 with ♕b1.

23 ...   gh   119

Grandmaster Tamas Georgadze, in charge of the bulletin here, has had very close links with the Karpov camp in the past. His comments may be taken as an authoritative indication of the drift of thought amongst Karpov's group in Seville. Here, for example, Georgadze mentions 23 ... ♔h7, continuing 24 ♕b3 ♘b6 25 ♕f7 ♘d5 26 hg ♕xg5 27 ♕f3 ♔g8, when he concludes that the situation is complex but still balanced.

24	♕b3	79	♕e6	120
25	♘f4	84		

If 25 ♗xh4 ♖f8 26 ♗xe7 ♖f1+ and White cannot capture since he would lose his queen to a knight check. Black's attack then is at least sufficient for a draw after 27 ♔h2.

25	...		♕f7	121
26	♘xg6	86	♕xg6	123
27	♕xc4+	86	♔h8	129
28	♖b2!	112		

A good move, seizing the b-file and preventing ... ♕b1+. Now Black had to consider 28 ... h3, since the line he chooses in the game leads to a disadvantage. 28 ... h3 sets a diabolical trap, namely 29 g3 ♗xe5 30 de ♖d1+ 31 ♔h2 ♖h1+ 32 ♔xh1 ♕c6+ and ... ♕g2 mate. In addition 29 ♗h4 is no good after 29 ... ♕h6, while 29 ♗e3 fails to 29 ... ♕e4 30 ♕e2 hg.

The best line is that indicated by the well-informed Georgadze: 28 ... h3 29 ♕f1 hg 30 ♕xg2 ♕xg2+

31 ♔xg2 and White has a very small endgame plus.

28	...		cd	135
29	cd	112	♕g4?	135

Kasparov's chief second, Josef Dorfman, said this was a terrible mistake by Kasparov, who had only fifteen minutes left on his clock to escape to the control at move 40. 29 ... h3 is still the best for Black, according to Dorfman. The lines would be analogous to 28 ... h3, but with the benefit for Black of the already open c-file.

30	♕f7!	119

Kasparov had clean overlooked this invasion and now he is obliged to sacrifice the exchange to stay alive.

30	...		♖xd4	142
31	♗xd4	122	♕xd4+	143
32	♖f2	122	♕xe5	143
33	♖f5	125	♕e1+	145
34	♖f1	125	♕e5	126
35	♔h1?	127		

White misses a chance in Black's clock trouble. Best is 35 ♕f4.

35	...		b6	146

A useful move, securing the queenside. If White's queen now goes marauding, the pawn to capture will be on a7, far from the scene of action.

36	♕f4	138

One move too late.

36	...		♕h5	146

For the moment Black must avoid the exchange of queens.

37	♕f5	139	♕e2	147
38	♖c1	141	♗f6	147
39	♕g6	141	♕e6	147
40	♖d1	145	♕c8	147
41	♖f1	147		

Surely it would have been more prudent to seal a move here.

41	...		♕d7	152
42	♕h5+?	149		

Karpov's sealed move. Clock times were about level here – ironic in a way since Karpov sealed quickly and threw away much of his advantage. Correct is 42 ♖c1 ♕e6 43 ♖d1 ♕c8 44 ♕h6+ ♔g8 45 ♖d5 and Black is still in a vice. 42 ♖f5 looks menacing but is drawn after 42 ... ♕d1+ 43 ♔h2 ♕d6+ 44 ♔h3 ♕d3+ 45 ♔g4 ♕e2+.

42	...		♔g7	156
43	♖f4	149	♕d2	160
44	♖g4+	150	♔f8	160
45	♕f5	150	♕c1+	168
46	♔h2	150	♕c7+	169
47	♕f4	156	♕xf4+	172

After the exchange of queens the ending is a positional draw.

Kasparov, however, is not content to sit in his fortress but chooses an incredibly sharp forcing line. This left Karpov stunned. From now until the end of the game Kasparov was moving quickly while Karpov fell further and further behind on the clock – around an hour at the end of play. Kasparov's team, Yeganov and Litvinov, gleefully crowding round the press room monitors, were actually claiming quite openly that it was all adjournment analysis. This seems incredible but may be true.

48	♖xf4	156	♔e8	172
49	♔g1	156	a6	181
50	♔f2	160	♔d7	186
51	♔e2	160	♔d6	190
52	♔d3	161	♔c5	199
53	♖c4+	168	♔d5	199

It would seem more sensible to play 53 ... ♔d6, denying White's rook access to the seventh rank and preparing ... b5 to liquidate the queenside pawns. If Black succeeds in trading all the pawns on the a- and b-files he will draw, even if he sheds a pawn in the process. Nevertheless, it is clear that passive defence was not in Kasparov's game plan for the second session.

54	♖c7	173	a5	199
55	♖c4	178	e5	199

If Karpov had been looking forward to an undemanding technical exercise in the second session he is now doomed to disappointment.

Instead of torturing Kasparov from a superior, if drawn ending, the challenger is forced to start calculating knife-edge variations.

56	♖g4	179	♗e7	200
57	♖g7	185	e4+	204
58	♔e3	188	♗c5+	206
59	♔e2	194	♗d4	212
60	♖g5+	223	♔c4	212
61	♖f5	238	♔c3	216

An important resource. If instead 61 ... ♔b3 62 ♖f4 ♗c5 63 ♖xe4 ♗b4 64 ♖xh4 ♔xa4 65 g4 and White wins.

62	♖h5	243	♔c4	216
63	♖f5	260	♔c3	216
64	♖g5	261	♔c4	217
65	♖h5	262	♗f6	218
66	♖b5	264	♗d4	219
67	♖h5	266	♗f6	221

Before playing this Kasparov approached the chief arbiter in the belief the position would be about to occur for the third time. This supposition turned out to be erroneous . . . so the band played on.

68	♖h6	269	♗d4	221
69	♖xh4	269	b5	222
70	ab	269	a4	222
71	♖xe4	269	a3	222
72	b6	269	a2	222

Here Karpov was flustered and unsure of how many moves had been made. As the time scramble ended Kasparov leant across and

pointed out to Karpov that he had made the time control at move 72.

73	♖xd4+	270	♔xd4	223
74	b7	270	a1♕	223
73	b8♕	273		

Karpov placed a new queen on b8 and removed his pawn from b7, instead of pushing the pawn to b8 and then replacing it with a fresh queen. This incredibly minor infringement of normal practice may seem trivial but it had the effect of nonplussing the match video display computer, which now stopped recording the moves.

75	...		♕a6+	223
76	♔f2	273	♕f6+	223
77	♔g1	273	♔e4	224
78	♕b4+	291	♔f5	224
79	♕e1	294	♕d4+	229

Draw Agreed

White plays 80 ♕f2+ and after the exchange of queens the king and pawn endgame is a draw.

| Kasparov | ½ 0 ½ 1 0 ½ ½ | 3 |
| Karpov | ½ 1 ½ 0 1 ½ ½ | 4 |

GAME EIGHT, 2 November

After long and patient positional manoeuvring, culminating in tactical fireworks, Kasparov notched up a second victory to level the score at 4-4.

From an English Opening Kasparov, playing White, gained an enduring positional advantage, with an iron grip on the light squares. Karpov set up a fortress-like blockade but, unable to improve his position, was reduced to marking time by moving a knight to and fro between a5 and b7.

Cynics who suggested the position might be adjourned without any real action had to eat their words. On his final move before adjournment, Kasparov thrust his f-pawn forward, threatening to blast a hole in Black's defensive wall.

Karpov spent 25 minutes pondering his sealed move, but failed to find the best course. The next day Kasparov produced a superb piece of overnight analysis that rocked grandmasters in the press room and forced surrender after only 42 minutes. At the moment her husband gave up, Natasha Karpova left the hall by a side entrance.

For Danish IM Bjarke Kristensen, the entire game had reminded him of ping-pong, the ball peacefully bouncing backwards and forwards over the net until Kasparov unleashed a series of killing smashes starting on move 42.

It was Eddie Gufeld who found the best way to describe Karpov's débâcle. The black knight, hobbling between its two squares on the queenside, as Kasparov crashed through on the kingside, had not been a mere spectator. For Gufeld, the black knight was a "witness for the prosecution".

Kasparov-Karpov				
English Opening				
1	c4	*00*	e5	*00*

2	♘c3	*00*	d6	*00*
3	g3	*02*	c5	*01*

An unusual move which weakens d5, but it is not necessarily bad.

| 4 | &g2 | 03 | &c6 | 02 |
| 5 | a3 | 09 | | |

The gambit 5 e3 g6 6 &ge2 &g7 7 0-0 &ge7 8 d4 looks very dangerous for Black, but he simply ignores it, viz: 8 ... ed 9 ed &g4 with a fully playable position.

| 5 | ... | | g6 | 07 |

Evans-Karpov, San Antonio 1972, opened 1 c4 c5 2 &c3 &c6 3 g3 g6 4 &g2 &g7 5 a3 d6 6 &b1 a5 7 &f3 e5 and Black obtained a satisfactory position. Perhaps the future world champion's idea of ... a5 was better than the plan adopted by the ex-champion.

| 6 | b4 | 12 | &g7 | 07 |

Karpov correctly avoids 6 ... cb 7 ab &xb4 8 &a4+ &c6 9 &xc6+ bc 10 &xc6+ &d7 11 &b7 and White exerts annoying pressure.

7	&b1	14	&ge7	07
8	e3	38	0-0	12
9	d3	43	&b8	33
10	&ge2	45	&e6	42
11	b5	55	&a5	42

Black's knight goes to the edge of the board and stays there transfixed more or less until the end of the game. This is reminiscent of a similar occurrence in game 19 of their second match, when Karpov's knight pinioned to a5 was the decisive factor in the game. Here, however, all is not yet lost by any means.

| 12 | &d2 | 57 | b6 | 48 |
| 13 | 0-0 | 61 | &b7 | 57 |

A frightfully passive move. Karpov should simply have played ... f5, when there should not be any cause for alarm in the Black camp. Unfortunately for Karpov, he seems to be obsessed by a bunker mentality throughout this game and ultimately pays the penalty for excessive caution. After 13 ... f5 14 e4? the tactical trick 14 ... f4! gives Black the advantage since if White captures on f4 his c3 knight hangs to the bishop on g7, while 14 f4 can be met by 14 ... e4!. White's best is probably 14 &d5 &xd5 15 cd, when 15 ... &d7 holds the balance – an interesting vindication of Black's apparently eccentric opening play.

14	e4	75	&h8	69
15	&c1	83	f5	74
16	&g5	89	&e8	79
17	&xe7	90		

All part of a deeply considered plan to seize control of the light squares across the board.

| 17 | ... | | &xe7 | 79 |

50

18 ef   92   ♗xf5?   86

Obviously a very weak move which betrays the fact that Karpov has never been a King's Indian player. He must, of course, as every Russian schoolboy should know, capture on f5 with the pawn. After this colossal strategic error Kasparov institutes a far-reaching blockade of the entire Black army.

After the correct 18 ... gf White plays 19 f4 and keeps the edge, but it would be nothing like the disaster which now overtakes the Black position.

19	♘d5	94	♕d7	87
20	♕d2	95	♘a5	94
21	♘ec3	97	♖be8	94
22	♘e4	102	♘b7	98
23	a4	102	♘a5	101

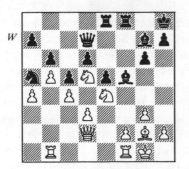

Black has to prevent White from rolling up his queen's wing with a5, which could even be played as an exchange sacrifice if Black were to leave his knight on b7. In the further course of the game Kasparov tries to win (and succeeds) by transfer-ring his pieces towards Black's king. Had this direct approach failed, White could always have reverted to the method of stationing one white knight on e4 and bringing the other one round to b3. That would ultimately have broken down Black's queenside barricades. As it happens, there is no need for this reserve action, since Karpov falls apart when the attack starts on the opposite wing.

24	h4	104	♘b7	106
25	♔h2	105	♖b8	108
26	♖a1	113	♘a5	108
27	♖a3	113		

White's manoeuvres are designed to stop Black from ever reintro-ducing his knight into the struggle with ... ♘b3 whilst simultaneously concentrating maximum force on the kingside. In the Spanish weekly *El Independiente*, IM Ricardo Calvo described Kasparov's conduct of the battle in this game as Napoleonic.

27	...		♖f7	111
28	♕c3	121	♖d8	114
29	♖a2	121	♗h6	117
30	♘g5	122	♖7f8	117
31	♖e2	122	♗g7	118

Rarely has Karpov been reduced to such utter helplessness.

32	♕c2	124	♖de8	119
33	♘e3	126	♗h6	123
34	♗d5	128	♗g7	127
35	♕d1	130	h6	129
36	♘e4	131	♕d8	133
37	♖a2	134	♗c8	137

| 38 | ♘c3 | *135* | h5 | *139* |

Karpov was obviously concerned that White would play h5 himself, but perhaps this is even more of a concession.

39	♗e4	*136*	♖e6	*139*
40	♘cd5	*139*	♗h6	*139*
41	♘g2	*141*	♔g7	*144*
42	f4	*152*		

Kasparov's mentor, Botvinnik, always taught that one should seal immediately given the option. Here Kasparov correctly breaks the rule, realising that Karpov will have a very difficult decision over his sealed move at the end of the first session. In fact Karpov spent around 25 minutes over his sealed move and made a poor one. When the game resumed next day Karpov was swiftly blown away without trace.

| 42 | ... | | ef | *170* |

? from Kasparov, who claimed 42 ... ♗b7 was best, when he intended to continue with 43 g4. I (RDK) won 1,000 pesetas from

Reuters correspondent Jon Tisdall who wagered that Karpov would resign overnight. I felt that Karpov's position was bad, but not that bad. Black's sealed move, however, does render his position resignable.

| 43 | ♘gxf4 | *154* | ♖e5 | *171* |

If 43 ... ♖xe4 44 de ♘xc4 45 ♖af2 with terrible threats of knight discoveries unleashing the battery of white rooks on the f-file. Probably the most tenacious, if miserably passive, defence is afforded by 43 ... ♗xf4 44 ♘xf4 ♖ef6 45 ♖af2 ♕d7 and now 46 ♕d2 virtually forces Black to sacrifice the exchange on f4, while the more patient 46 ♗g2 piles up threats and adds the unpleasant possibility of ♗h3. No wonder Karpov could not stomach this. His only way out might have been the inaccurate 46 ♔g1?, when 46 ... ♕g4 47 ♕xg4 ♗xg4 48 ♘xg6 ♖xf2 49 ♖xf2 ♖e8! threatens ... ♖xe4 and ... ♘xc4. It would, however, have been imprudent to rely on this eventuality.

Instead Karpov tries an ingenious defence, but he had clearly missed the combination Kasparov now unleashes. Kasparov moved almost instantly from now to the end of the game, while Karpov was rooted to the board, desperately trying to find a means of salvation.

44	♘xg6	*154*	♖xf1	*173*
45	♕xf1	*155*	♖xe4	*176*
46	de	*157*	♔xg6	*178*

47 ♖f2 *158*

For a modest material investment (remember the knight is still stuck on a5) all of White's pieces pour into a devastating mating attack. This is just the kind of bravura tactics the public love to see from Kasparov.

47 ... ♕e8 *190*

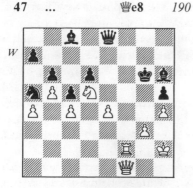

Or 47 ... ♗g7 48 ♖f7 and Black is helpless.

48 e5!! *160*

Another crushing blow. If 48 ... ♕xe5 49 ♖e2 wins. Black must take with the pawn, when he no longer has e5 available for his queen. This brilliant move is the key to White's victory.

48 ... de *193*
49 ♖f6+ *160* **♔g7** *196*
50 ♖d6 *161* **Resigns**

If 50 ... ♗d2 51 ♕f6+ and 52 ♖d8, or 50 ... ♕f7 (50 ... ♕f8 meets the same fate) 51 ♕xf7+ and 52 ♖xh6.

I once described Karpov as an atomic Capablanca – in this game Kasparov reminds me of a nuclear-powered Petrosian.

Kasparov	½	0	½	1	0	½	½	1	4
Karpov	½	1	½	0	1	½	½	0	4

GAME NINE, 4 November

Despite his loss in game 8, Karpov came to the Lope de Vega theatre the following afternoon in aggressive mood.

Following their now familiar variation in the Grünfeld, Kasparov was the first to innovate. But the champion's idea proved less than successful and Karpov, gaining space in the centre, seized the initiative in the middlegame.

On move 25 Karpov forced the black king out onto the wrong side of its defensive wall of pawns. For the next fifteen moves it had to survive life on the front line as Karpov sought to deliver the *coup de grâce* (which came to light only after the game).

Before play resumed a consensus emerged that Kasparov would hold, though he might have to suffer first. But once in the second session Kasparov flicked out a clever pawn sacrifice which removed any winning chances White may have had.

After the early games Kasparov adopted a new strategy as regards his seconds. Instead of roaming the press centre during play, they stayed at home, conserving their energy for the long nights of analysis and preparation. Given that the Kasparov camp had just out-analysed Karpov's team three games in succession, it did not look like a bad idea.

Karpov-Kasparov
Grünfeld Defence

1	d4	00	♘f6	01	8	♘e2	00	♘c6	03
2	c4	00	g6	02	9	♗e3	01	0-0	04
3	♘c3	00	d5	02	10	0-0	01	♗g4	07
4	cd	00	♘xd5	03	11	f3	01	♘a5	07
5	e4	00	♘xc3	03	12	♗xf7+	01	♖xf7	08
6	bc	00	♗g7	03	13	fg	01	♖xf1+	08
7	♗c4	00	c5	03	14	♔xf1	01		

IM William Watson described this as a modern *tabia*, a parallel to the old Arabic version of chess

54

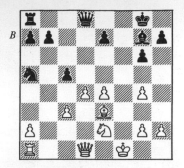

where play proceeded from certain standard middlegame positions.

| 14 | ... | cd | 08 |

A new departure, clearing lines in the centre and offering transposition to earlier known games. I (RDK) had believed that Karpov's idea was to meet this delayed capture with 15 ♗xd4, but the former champion did not pause for long before proving me wrong.

| 15 | cd | 02 | ♛b6 | 08 |

A novelty. Well established alternatives are 15 ... ♛d7 16 h3 ♛c6 17 ♛d3 ♛c4 (first played over thirty years ago in Spassky-Korchnoi, USSR Championship 1955) and 15 ... ♛d6 16 ♔g1 ♛e6 17 ♘g3 ♖d8, both of which are quoted as equal for Black in the Yugoslav *Encyclopaedia*. Karpov's improved method of interpreting this line is based on the insight that White does not have to cling religiously to the corbel of his position on g4 but can give it back to gain time and space in the centre.

| 16 | ♔g1 | 13 | ♛e6 | 10 |
| 17 | ♛d3! | 14 | | |

A tremendous move, clearly studied before the game. Yeganov, Kasparov's head of delegation, said to me: "There has been much home preparation for this game – for that reason I call it the battle of the houses."

In contrast, the feeble 17 ♘g3 transposes to the line given as equal in the Yugoslav text. Black must now expend time with his queen to re-establish material parity.

17	...		♛xg4	12
18	♖f1	17	♖c8	20
19	h3	30	♛d7	21
20	d5	30		

Black's difficulties become crystal clear. White threatens to play ♘d4 and ♘e6, which gives him a terrible initiative, even if Black manages to trade the last pair of rooks. Another threat is ♗d4 eliminating the g7 bishop, the minder of the black king.

Kasparov thought long and hard over his next two moves. An error here would be instantly fatal.

| 20 | ... | | ♘c4 | 36 |
| 21 | ♗d4 | 53 | e5 | 69 |

An unpleasant move to make and not the best, though the refutation is not easy to find. In any case, the alternative 21 ... ♘e5 is also unappetising, as can be seen from analysis by the well-connected

55

Georgadze in the bulletin: 21 ... ♘e5 22 ♕g3 ♕d6 23 ♕b3 or 22 ♗xe5 ♗xe5 23 ♘d4 ♗xd4+ 24 ♕xd4 b6 25 e5 ♕c7 26 ♕g4. All of this looks nasty for Black, but not as hideous as the game could have been.

22	de	67	♕xe6	69
23	♗xg7	67	♔xg7	69
24	♘f4	68	♕d6	70
25	♕c3+	72	♔h6	70

W

Black's last move was forced, for if 25 ... ♕e5 26 ♘e6+ ♔h6 27 ♕c1+ g5 28 ♘xg5 ♕xg5 29 ♖f6+ ♔h5 30 ♕d1+ ♔h4 31 ♖h6+ ♕xh6 32 ♕g4 mate. Alternatively, 26 ... ♔g8 27 ♕xc4 ♖xc4 28 ♖f8 mate.

So, 25 ... ♔h6 is the most tenacious defence, but it would have been quite inadequate if Karpov had paused to think for more than a few minutes before banging out his next move.

In fact, in the diagrammed position White can win with 26 ♘d3!!. This retrograde move may look odd but the point is to break Black's control of the e5 square, which is the cornerstone of his entire defensive operation. Instead of this Karpov plays an apparently more aggressive move which commits his knight, a key attacking unit, to the wrong circuit.

After 26 ♘d3!! White threatens ♖f7 and ♘f2-g4, and this combination is ultimately unstoppable, e.g. 26 ... ♖c7 27 ♘f2 ♘e5 28 ♕xe5 ♕xe5 29 ♘g4+, or 26 ... ♘b6 27 ♕d2+ ♔g7 28 ♕b2+ ♔g8 29 ♕b3+ ♔h8 30 ♖f7 and the optimum Black can hope for is a miserable endgame a pawn down.

| 26 | ♘d5? | 78 | ♕e5 | 73 |

Black's defence is precarious, but it holds in all variations once White's knight has wandered off target.

| 27 | ♕d3 | 86 | | |

If 27 ♕b4 ♘d6 28 ♘f6 ♕c5+ 29 ♕xc5 ♖xc5 30 ♖d1 ♖c6 is level.

| 27 | ... | | ♔g7 | 85 |
| 28 | ♘f6 | 89 | ♕d6 | 88 |

Timman pointed out one brilliant way for Black to go down in flames: 28 ... ♔h8? 29 ♕d7 ♕c7 30 ♘e8 ♕xd7 31 ♖f8 mate. But after his fortunate earlier escape Kasparov consistently finds the best defence.

29	♕c3	99	♕e5	88
30	♕d3	105	♕d6	89
31	♕c3	106	♕e5	89
32	♕b3	107	♖c7	97
33	♕d3	128		

Karpov is running out of steam

– White's position cannot be improved.

33	...		♖f7	98
34	♕xc4	135	♖xf6	98
35	♖d1	135		

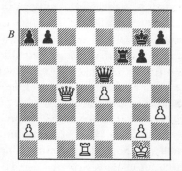

A sign of fighting spirit. Instead Karpov could have offered a draw which would doubtless have been accepted.

| 35 | ... | | b5 | 106 |

Another fascinating moment. The logic of the position is that it has burnt out – a draw is not only evident but surely imminent. However, Karpov tried to keep a flicker of life going with his last move, and now Kasparov reciprocates. Of course, after 35 ... ♖e6 36 ♖d7+ ♖e7 37 ♖xe7+ ♕xe7 38 ♕d4+ ♔f7 39 ♕xa7 ♕xe4 the position is totally drawn, and White does not have anything better in this line.

Kasparov's 35th move is objectively worse than this, but it keeps the battle going. Its concept reminds me of many Lasker games, or perhaps Fischer's famous (and more

risky) 29 ... ♗xh2 in game 1 against Spassky in 1972.

| 36 | ♖d7+ | 137 | ♔h6 | 106 |
| 37 | ♕e2 | 138 | ♕c5+ | 124 |

The time consumed over this last move indicates that Kasparov sensed he might have pushed too much. His king is now a little awkward on h6, while White's rook on the 7th rank may one day glean a pawn.

| 38 | ♔h2 | 141 | ♕e5+ | 125 |
| 39 | g3 | 143 | | |

Karpov plays exquisitely to cover his own king from checks, simultaneously avoiding the exchange of queens, which would normally eliminate his prospects of a win. Nevertheless, Black has still not overstepped the boundary of the draw.

39	...		♕c3	134
40	♔g2	146	♕c4	135
41	♕e3+	149	g5	136
42	♖d2	150	♕f1+	143

Both players sail on without deigning to seal a move.

| 43 | ♔h2 | 154 | | |

Here Kasparov finally sealed a move. His situation has once again become precarious – there is a distinct danger of his being squeezed to death. But on resumption a forcing line of play made the draw clear.

43 ...   ♛f3   154
44 ♛d4   154

To retain any winning chances at all White must keep queens on the board.

44 ...   ♖e6   154

Attacking White's passed e-pawn and firmly blockading it before it can advance and inflict further damage.

45 e5   155

45 ♖f2? fails to 45 ... ♛xe4 46 ♖f6+ ♚g7 and White loses a pawn without having any dangerous discovered checks.

45 ...   ♛f5   154

Increasingly tying White to the e-pawn.

46 ♖e2   156 a5!   154

An outstanding method of active

defence, quite in Kasparov's effervescent style. Many players would sit and dig in with a move like ... a6 but then there is some danger of being slowly and remorselessly strangled by the Karpovian python technique after 47 ♚g2 and g4, or even 47 g4 at once. Kasparov's line rules out such perils of attrition and forces Karpov to go hunting pawns if he wants to win. It should be pointed out that Karpov (as in games 7 and 8) seemed surprised by Kasparov's confident handling of the adjourned position. Georgadze, doubtless privy to some of Karpov's conclusions, cites another variation for Black to avoid, viz: 46 ... ♚g6 47 g4 ♛f4+ 48 ♛xf4 (now it is OK to trade queens since White has a target to annex) 48 ... gf 49 ♚g2 a5 50 ♚f3 b4 51 ♚xf4 a4 52 ♖e4 ♖b6 53 e6 and White wins.

47 ♛d5

After this the draw speedily becomes clear as Black's forces assume dominant posts in the centre of the board. But if White tries to win as in the above note we can see the tempo-gaining value of Black's ... a5: 47 g4 ♛f4+ 48 ♛xf4 gf 49 ♚g2 b4 50 ♚f3 a4 51 ♚xf4 b3 52 ab ab with a draw. Alternatively in this line: 50 ♖e4 ♚g7 51 ♚f3 ♖b6 52 e6 ♖b8 and again Black holds on.

47 ...   b4
48 ♛xa5

58

Or 48 g4 ♕f7 49 ♕xa5 ♕f3 50 ♕b5 ♖c6 51 ♖b2 ♕f4+ 52 ♔g2 ♕e4+, also drawing.

48	...	♕d3	
49	♖g2	♕d4	
50	♕a8	♕xe5	
51	♕f8+	♔g6	
52	♕xb4	*163*	h5	*158*

The last difficult move. Black plans to ram forward his h-pawn to further reduce the shelter around the white king. Meanwhile, White's extra a-pawn, isolated and on the edge, can play little role in proceedings.

53	h4	*172*	gh	*159*
54	♕xh4	*172*	♖d6	*170*
55	♕c4	*186*	♖d4	*170*
56	♕c6+	*197*	♔g7	*181*
57	♕b7+	*199*	♔h6	*183*
58	♕c6+	*208*	♔g7	*184*

| 59 | ♖c2 | *209* | ♖h4+ | |

A neat way to eliminate the queens and transpose into a dead drawn rook and pawn ending.

| 60 | ♔g2 | ♕e4+ | |
| 61 | ♕xe4 | ♖xe4 | |

This ending is a well-known theoretical draw and it is quite surprising that White plays on. There is only one trap worth noting – the black king has to be on g7 (not f7) when White's a-pawn gets to a7, otherwise the white rook can jump to h8 and skewer on h7. Since this device is known to most schoolchildren who learn chess there was not much point seeing if the world champion was aware of it.

62	♖c7+		♔g6	*188*
63	♖a7	*210*	♖e3	
64	♔h3	*211*	♖c3	
65	♖a8	*212*	♖c4	*192*
66	a4		♔g5	

A small tease, but as White's a-pawn advances Kasparov rushes his king back to g7.

| 67 | a5 | | ♖a4 | |

Rook behind the passed pawn.

68	a6		♔h6	
69	♔g2		♖a3	
70	♔f2		♔g7	

Draw Agreed

| Kasparov | ½ | 0 | ½ | 1 | 0 | ½ | ½ | 1 | ½ | 4½ |
| Karpov | ½ | 1 | ½ | 0 | 1 | ½ | ½ | 0 | ½ | 4½ |

GAME TEN, 6 November

The spectators' spirits rose – indeed there was a round of applause – when Kasparov played a king's pawn opening for the first time in the match. But hopes of a good clean fight were quickly dashed when Karpov responded with the Caro-Kann. Usually he had accepted the challenge of an open game in world championships, but not this time.

Kasparov-Karpov
Caro-Kann Defence

1	e4	00			

At last a king's pawn opening.

1	...	c6	00		

Karpov replies with the super-safe Caro-Kann, which he had used so effectively in the Candidates final against Sokolov.

2	d4	00	d5	00
3	♘d2	00	de	00
4	♘xe4	00	♘d7	00
5	♘f3	01	♘gf6	01
6	♘xf6+	01	♘xf6	01
7	c3			

Sokolov twice tried 7 ♘e5 against Karpov, but could make no headway.

7	...		♗g4	14
8	h3	02	♗xf3	14
9	♕xf3	02	e6	17
10	♗c4	06	♗e7	23

11	0-0	08	♘d5	24

This vigorous move finally gives White pause for thought.

12	♗e3	26	♕b6	43
13	♕e2	29	0-0	44
14	♖ad1	29	♗d6	52
15	♗b3	62		

In meeting Black's active defence White cedes his lead on the clock. If 15 ♗c1 ♗f4! 16 ♗xd5 ♗xc1 threatening ... ♕xb2.

15	...		♘xe3	66
16	fe	63	c5	66
17	♖f3	75	♖ae8	74
18	♖df1	91	♖e7	75
19	♕f2	93	♕c7	84
20	♕h4	95	**Draw Agreed**	

Both players seemed drained by their exertions in games 7, 8 and 9. But Karpov clearly has the Caro-Kann well sewn up. It will be interesting to see if Kasparov can find a way of unstitching it in this match.

Kasparov	½ 0 ½ 1 0 ½ ½ 1 ½ ½	5
Karpov	½ 1 ½ 0 1 ½ ½ 0 ½ ½	5

GAME ELEVEN, 9 November

One of the worst mistakes in world championship history – "the blunder of the century" in one verdict.

For Kasparov it was a wonderful gift to mark the anniversary of 9 November 1985, the day on which he became the youngest world chess champion in history. For Karpov it was "Black Monday". Another coincidence did not escape the notice of informed observers. It was also in game 11 of the 1985 match that Karpov had committed a major error, permitting Kasparov to win with a queen sacrifice. There were some who found the way history was repeating itself just a little eerie. "Maybe it's black magic", said Ljubomir Ljubojević.

A pawn ahead and playing for a win, Karpov had left himself more than 27 minutes to make only six moves. But he only thought for one minute before playing his fatal 35th.

When Kasparov saw the blunder, he seemed unable to control his reactions. He leaned back in his chair, shook his head and began to make faces. He brought up his right hand to cover a broad grin. Moments after capturing the white rook, he raised his right hand above his shoulder with the first and fourth fingers pointing up; the twist of the wrist that followed was like a matador flourishing his cape.

Karpov fought on, the exchange down, and Kasparov spent 35 minutes over his sealed move. A shattered Karpov held on for only fifteen minutes the next day. The "Seville Variation" of the Grünfeld had rebounded on Karpov who, sensing victory, had lost his concentration with his impetuous rook manoeuvre.

As challenger, Karpov now required not one but two victories to take the title.

Karpov-Kasparov	1	d4	00	♘f6	01
Grünfeld Defence	2	c4	00	g6	01

3   ♘c3   00   d5   01

Yet another Grünfeld Defence. The time has come to explain who the newly popular Herr Grünfeld was. Ernst Grünfeld (1893-1962) was an Austrian grandmaster noted for his logical style and theoretical acumen. Active in the 1920s, he was a dangerous opponent for anyone and launched the defence which bears his name with a convincing win against the mighty Alekhine.

When did Kasparov first feel attracted towards the Grünfeld? Dorfman, the world champion's chief second, has revealed that it was studied as an emergency weapon for the crucial game 24 of the 1985 match which brought Kasparov the title. Kasparov had been suffering on the Black side of the Queen's Gambit and was in need of a new defence for that final game. As it was, Karpov chose 1 e4 and went on to lose on the White side of a Sicilian.

4	cd	00	♘xd5	01
5	e4	00	♘xc3	01
6	bc	00	♗g7	01
7	♗c4	01	c5	01
8	♘e2	01	♘c6	01
9	♗e3	01	0-0	02
10	0-0	01	♗g4	02
11	f3	01	♘a5	02
12	♗xf7+	02	♖xf7	03
13	fg	02	♖xf1+	03
14	♔xf1	02	♕d6	03

Kasparov reverts to his treatment from games 5 and 7 after his near débâcle in game 9. Grandmaster Mark Taimanov complained that the match was turning into a doctoral dissertation on the Grünfeld rather than a fight for the world title.

15   ♔g1   03

A new move, varying from the 15 e5 of games 5 and 7. Karpov is clearly hoping to transpose into the continuation of game 5, which was favourable for White. Kasparov, naturally, does not oblige.

15   ...   ♕e6   04

Kasparov postpones ... cd and plays this move not only with the thought of capturing on g4 but with the deeper positional intention of occupying the weak c4 square.

16   ♕d3   11

Still angling for transposition, which could follow on 16 ... cd 17 cd ♕xg4 etc. In the bulletin Tamas Georgadze, with one ear in the

62

Karpov camp perhaps, adorns 16 ♕d3 with "!?" and no further note, implying there is a stronger move, but not wishing to reveal what it is. Perhaps this will surface in a later game in this hotly debated line.

16	...	♕c4!	*04*
17	♕xc4+	*11*	♘xc4	*04*
18	♗f2	*14*		

Keeping the bishop in touch with the sensitive d4 pawn. If 18 ♗c1 cd 19 cd e5 20 d5 ♗f8 21 ♗g5 h6 22 ♗f6 ♗c5+ 23 ♔h1 ♖f8 24 g5 ♗e3 25 ♗e7 ♖f7 26 d6 ♗xg5, undermining the support of the passed d-pawn. It is important to note the role of the move ... e5 in Black's counterplay. It cedes White a passed d-pawn and also blocks the a1-h8 diagonal, but it has the virtue of establishing a choice of two other key diagonals for Black's bishop, c1-h6 and a3-f8.

| 18 | ... | cd | *04* |
| 19 | cd | *14* | e5 | *04* |

A further plus side to ... e5 is the setting up of d6 as a base for the black knight.

| 20 | d5 | *16* | ♗h6 | *15* |

The bishop promptly seizes the important diagonal and Karpov takes countermeasures to shut it out of play.

| 21 | h4 | *21* | ♗d2 | *18* |

Necessary, before White slides the bolt with g5.

| 22 | ♖d1 | *41* | | |

This natural move seemed to surprise Kasparov, who invested 29 minutes in his reply. With ♖d1 White is toying with such ideas as ♘c1 and perhaps the tactical shot d6. In fact, neither of these is dangerous and Black should now have played the consistent and strong 22 ... b5!. If 23 ♘c1 a5 24 ♘b3 ♗b4 followed by the advance of Black's queenside pawn majority. In comparison with this asset White's extra pawn, doubled and on the other wing, is irrelevant. Dorfman claimed that Black would have been at least equal after 22 ... b5!.

Similarly, if 22 ... b5 23 d6 then 23 ... a5 followed by ... ♖d8 and Black will simply round up the white d-pawn, which has wandered too far beyond its own lines of communication.

| 22 | ... | ♗a5? | *47* |
| 23 | ♖c1 | *51* | | |

Black's bishop retreat was not just a wasted move, it had the additional unpleasant side effect

63

of making the excellent c1 square available for White's rook.

| 23 | ... | **b5** | *67* |

This is now risky. In the press room Taimanov gave 22 ... ♘d6 23 ♘g3 ♗b6 24 ♗xb6 ab 25 ♖c7 ♖a4 26 ♖d7 ♘xe4 with equality.

24	♖c2	*64*	♘d6	*69*
25	♘g3	*65*	♘c4	*69*
26	♘f1	*72*	♘d6	*84*
27	♘g3	*81*	♘c4	*84*
28	g5	*86*		

Karpov quite rightly elects to continue the struggle rather than accede to a draw by repetition. The text is an excellent choice that set Kasparov thinking for a further 38 minutes. The point is that White nails down f6 as a future point for invasion, especially by a knight travelling via f1-h2-g4.

| 28 | ... | ♔f7 | *122* |

The time consumed here is an admission that Black's position is exceedingly difficult. Nevertheless, this move is the starting point for a profound trap, which Kasparov later confirmed was intentional.

Surprisingly, he even indicated that he had been half expecting Karpov to fall into the additional trap of placing his rook on c6: "If you play ♖f6 you are obviously planning to continue with ♖c6."

29	♘f1	*102*	♘d6	*122*
30	♘g3	*115*	♘c4	*122*
31	♔f1	*115*		

Again Karpov rejects the draw and sets off with his king towards d3, its optimum post.

| 31 | ... | ♔e7!! | *128* |

A brilliant defensive trap, quite in the style of that tenacious old defender Emanuel Lasker. When Kasparov played this move the immediate reaction of all grandmasters present was that it was a terrible blunder, allowing White to play ♗c5+ and ♖f2 with decisive gain of tempo. In fact, this is just what Kasparov wanted. By racing his pieces to these apparently crushing invasion squares (which Karpov did without much thought, also convinced that Kasparov had blundered under pressure) White loses cohesion amongst his entire army. Instead of his next move White should just have proceeded with his king journey to d3.

32 &c5+ *116* **&f7** *133*

Of course, 32 ... &d7 really does lose to 33 &f2, so Black's king must retrace its steps. Kasparov accompanied this retreat with what Reuters correspondent Jon Tisdall described as a "decidedly theatrical . . . assortment of grimaces" – presumably designed to display overt dissatisfaction with his prospects. Although the inspired defence in this game is Laskerian, I doubt that the old master would have accompanied his moves with such theatrical gestures.

33 &f2+ *117* **&g7** *133*
34 &f6 *123*

White ploughs ever deeper into the mire. Georgadze suggested that 34 h5 would have been stronger, but Karpov was still under the powerful delusion that he was dictating the course of events.

34 ... **&b6** *134*

Black's last move was excellent, exploiting the fact that White's bishop is no longer protected. If now, for example, 35 &xb6 ab 36 &f2 (one disadvantage of 34 &f6: the a-pawn lacks protection) then both 36 ... &a3 and 36 ... &a4 are well playable. White should play the humble 35 &f2, when Black can speculate with 35 ... &e3+ or head for a general liquidation with 35 ... &f8 36 &xf8 &xf8 37 &xb6 &xb6. In the knight and pawn ending Black is fine. White's passed d-pawn is heavily blockaded, while Black's queenside pawn majority is fully the equal of White's stymied pawn mass on the other wing.

Instead, after a mere minute of thought, Karpov produces the most horrendous blunder of his world championship career. Dominic Lawson, here in Seville for the *Spectator*, even went so far as to describe it as the "blunder of the century".

35 &c6??? *124*

It is to Karpov's immense credit that having made one of the worst moves of his life he did not bat an eyelid, but continued as if nothing untoward had happened.

35 ... **&a5** *134*

This wins the exchange in broad daylight. Perhaps Karpov had forgotten that knights can also jump backwards towards the edge, a mental image reinforced by the incessant pendulum-like movement of the black knight between c4 and d6.

More theatrics accompanied this devastating blow. It seemed that Kasparov literally could not believe his eyes. "As Kasparov reached out to make the killing move his hand darted back and forth like the head of a cobra. Afterwards his eyes bulged, his hand shot to his mouth to cover a broad grin and he leaned back, shaking his head in bemused disbelief." That was how this bizarre scene struck Jon Tisdall.

Georgadze could also not restrain himself from some purple passages in the bulletin. "Kasparov . . . remained completely confused . . . he did not reply at once and it was interesting to observe the expression on his face which changed every second. He was smiling and showing the rejoicing a person may feel who sees how Fortune smiles for him."

36   ♗xb6   125

There is no choice. Karpov must rely on his extra pawn and Black's generally congested position to give him compensation for the lost exchange.

36	...	♘xc6	134
37	♗c7	125	♖f8+	140
38	♔e2	126

If 38 ♘f5+ gf 39 dc fe+ 40 ♔e2 ♖e8 wins.

| 38 | ... | ♖f7 | 140 |

39	♗d6	126	♖d7	140
40	♗c5	128	♘a5	141
41	♘f1	139

Here Kasparov had to seal a move and he took 33 minutes over it. The position is won but demands some accurate play. White, if given time, may transfer his knight to f6 and there will always be problems with the weak pawn on e5, prone to attack from White's bishop. Kasparov, in fact, finds the most deadly method of terminating the game. 41 ... ♘c4 is rather slow, allowing 42 ♘h2 followed by ♘g4-h6, causing all sorts of difficulties. 41 ... ♘b7 (recommended by Ljubojević) sets a neat trap: 42 ♗xa7 ♘d6 43 ♗b8 ♘f7 threatening ... ♖b7. If White does not play 43 ♗b8 he loses his e-pawn for no compensation. However, White has a better defence, Georgadze's 42 ♗a3 and then ♗b2.

Kasparov's method cuts through all this and is simplest and best.

| 41 | ... | ♖c7 | 174 |

66

The black rook will penetrate immediately to mop up White's queenside pawns. White can create connected passed pawns in the centre but they are helpless against correct analysis. Indeed the second session only lasted for a few minutes – both sides knew the game was up once Kasparov had found the right sealed move.

42	♗d6		♖c2+
43	♔d3		♖xa2
44	♘e3		

It makes no difference whether this is played now or whether White first captures on e5.

| 44 | ... | | ♔f7 |
| 45 | ♘g4 | 140 | |

If 45 ♗xe5 ♖a3+ 46 ♔e2 ♖a4 47 ♔d3 ♘b3 wins.

45	...		♘c4	175
46	♘xe5+	141	♘xe5+	
47	♗xe5	141	b4	176
48	♗f6	146		

Trying to control the promotion square, but the black pawns are faster.

| 48 | ... | | b3 | 176 |
| 49 | e5 | 147 | | |

If 49 ♔c3 then 49 ... ♖e2 wins.

| 49 | ... | | ♖xg2 | 177 |

Naturally not 49 ... b2? 50 ♔c2 holding the pawn.

| 50 | e6+ | 147 | ♔f8 | 177 |

White Resigns

There is no defence to ... b2. Great and resourceful defence by Kasparov but a tragedy for Karpov.

| Kasparov | ½ 0 ½ 1 0 ½ ½ 1 ½ ½ 1 | 6 |
| Karpov | ½ 1 ½ 0 1 ½ ½ 0 ½ ½ 0 | 5 |

67

GAME TWELVE, 11 November

The twelfth game ended tamely after a mere 21 moves. The board was crowded with pieces and an interesting middlegame appeared in prospect when Kasparov offered a draw. Karpov, after pondering a few minutes, accepted. The explanation may have been that both players were drained after their exertions in the dramatic eleventh game.

So at the halfway stage Kasparov leads, as last year, by six and a half points to five and a half. Botvinnik opined before the 1985 match that Kasparov would be doing well if he were equal or one behind by the middle of the match. In 1985 that proved prophetic, but no one is likely to forget Karpov's extraordinary revival from apparently certain defeat at Leningrad last year. In the second half of this match both men still have everything to play for.

Kasparov-Karpov
Queen's Gambit Declined

1	c4	00	e6	00		15	♘ge2	65	♖ac8	89		
2	♘c3	00	d5	00		16	♕d2	74	♘h5	93		
3	d4	00	♗e7	00		17	♗h2	75	♘g7	94		
4	cd	01	ed	00		18	g4	81	♕d8	98		
5	♗f4	01	♘f6	01		19	f3	86	♘b6	101		
6	e3	02	♗f5	02		20	b3	88	♗a3	102		
7	♘ge2	09	0-0	07		21	♖c2	97	**Draw Agreed**			
8	♖c1	12	c6	18								
9	♘g3	13	♗e6	25								
10	♗d3	14	♖e8	45								
11	♕b3	24	♕b6	47								
12	♕c2	25	♘bd7	50								
13	0-0	26	g6	57								
14	h3	49	♗f8	69								

Kasparov	½	0	½	1	0	½	½	1	½	½	1	½	6½
Karpov	½	1	½	0	1	½	½	0	½	½	0	½	5½

68

GAME THIRTEEN, 13 November

As the thirteenth game – and the second half of the match – began, a fight broke out among spectators waiting in a line at the Casino de la Exposición, separated from the playing hall by just one door. The pushing, shoving and shouting came from fans anxious to get their hands on one of the last pairs of earphones, enabling them to listen to the running game commentary by Ljubojević. Indeed, the devices were to prove especially useful for this game, arguably the most accurately played so far.

Playing White, Karpov decided to rest his "Seville Variation" and hoped to blow away Kasparov's Grünfeld with a Modern Exchange Variation. But the title-holder had obviously come well prepared for this eventuality and his chosen system left Karpov pondering his 21st move for 49 minutes, the challenger's longest think of the match so far.

When they agreed a draw Kasparov was clearly disappointed with his failure to gain the full point. Frustrated, the champion rushed out of the theatre, missing a scheduled interview with Spanish TV.

Perhaps Kasparov had been expecting to win this thirteenth game, played on Friday 13th. Born on 13 April and the thirteenth world champion in history, this is his lucky number. Some people suggested that Karpov might take a time-out to avoid playing on Kasparov's "lucky day". Though superstitious too, Karpov is far too level-headed to throw away a time-out. (Anyway, in Spain it is Tuesday 13th that is considered unlucky, not Friday.)

Deeper analysis of the game over the next few days revealed that Kasparov had not, in fact, missed any chances to extend his lead. Karpov had played brilliantly to remain only one point adrift. On the other hand, it was the second time in a row that Kasparov had achieved a comfortable equality with Black.

Karpov-Kasparov
Grünfeld Defence

1	d4	*00*	♘f6	*00*
2	c4	*00*	g6	*00*
3	♘c3	*00*	d5	*01*
4	♘f3	*00*		

Karpov abandons the Classical Exchange Variation against the Grünfeld. It soon transpires that he still wants to use an exchange line, but a more modern version with the white knight on f3. From this decision it can be inferred that, at least for the moment, Kasparov has won the theoretical duel which extended through games 5-11.

4	...		♗g7	*01*
5	cd	*02*	♘xd5	*01*
6	e4	*02*	♘xc3	*01*
7	bc	*02*	c5	*01*
8	♖b1	*02*	0-0	*04*
9	♗e2	*03*	cd	*05*
10	cd	*03*	♕a5+	*05*

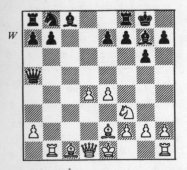

| 11 | ♕d2 | *03* | | |

Rejecting the more speculative 11 ♗d2 ♕xa2 12 0-0 b6 13 ♕c1 ♕e6 14 ♗c4 ♕xe4 15 ♖e1 ♕b7 16 ♗b4, when White has nebulous compensation for his sacrificed pawns.

11	...		♕xd2+	*05*
12	♗xd2	*03*	e6	*17*
13	0-0	*05*	b6	*17*

At this juncture 14 ♖bc1 is common, e.g. 14 ... ♗b7 15 ♗b4 ♖d8 16 ♗b5 ♗f8 with approximate equality. Karpov tries for more.

14	♖fd1	*07*	♗b7	*19*
15	d5	*08*		

Introducing the strategic theme of the entire variation – White's central pawn majority will yield a passed d-pawn. The question is, will this pawn be a murderous battering ram or a liability tying White down to its defence? The answer, after some brilliant play by both sides, lies somewhere in between.

15	...		ed	*19*
16	ed	*08*	♘d7	*21*
17	♗b4	*09*	♖fc8	*22*

Apart from the line Karpov now chooses two other possibilities are known to theory: 18 ♗b5 ♘f6 19 d6 ♘d5 and now 20 d7 ♖d8 21 ♖xd5 ♗xd5 22 ♗e7 h6, and White made no appreciable gains in Miralles-Korchnoi, Cannes 1986, or 20 ♘d4 ♘xb4 21 d7 ♖c5 22 ♖xb4 ♖d5, when Black is likewise OK, Lputian-Tukmakov, USSR 1985.

| 18 | ♗e7 | *10* | ♗f6! | *57* |

A startling indication of the extent of modern theory – this is the first new move. 18 ... ♗f8 is known from a game played by two juniors in England last year. Wells-Wolff, Oakham 1986, had gone 18 ... ♗f8 19 d6 ♗xe7 20 de ♘f6 21 ♗b5 ♔g7 22 ♘e5 a6, and presumably Karpov felt quite confident about this line.

19	**d6**	*13*	**♔g7**	*65*
20	**♖e1**	*62*		

Karpov spent 49 minutes on this move. If 20 ♗b5 ♗c6 21 ♗a6 ♖e8 22 ♘d4 ♗a4, when the threat against White's rook disrupts his initiative.

20	**...**		**♖c5**	*75*
21	**♗b5**	*71*	**♗c6**	*84*
22	**♗xc6**	*80*	**♖xc6**	*84*
23	**♖bd1**	*80*	**♗c3**	*85*

By harassing White's rook, Kasparov hopes to gain time to isolate the white bishop on e7.

| 24 | **♖e3** | *83* | | |

Karpov later stated that 24 ♖e4 would have been stronger.

24	**...**		**f6**	*91*
25	**g4**	*90*		

Starting an operation to rescue his bishop, currently stranded and locked in on e7.

25	**...**		**g5**	*93*
26	**h4**	*104*	**h6**	*94*
27	**hg**	*112*		

Here 27 ♖c1 ♖ac8 28 ♗d8 would already draw. Karpov demonstrated the following line: 28 ... ♖xd8 29 ♖cxc3 ♖xd6 30 ♖e7+ ♔g8 31 ♖c7 and White's activity guarantees that he will never lose. Karpov added, though, that he did not yet want to "run for the draw" in this fashion.

| 27 | **...** | | **hg** | *94* |

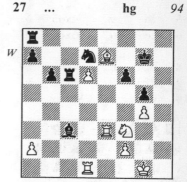

| 28 | **♘d4** | *116* | | |

This was universally condemned by the back-seat grandmasters in the press room, with 28 ♖d5 being given as best. But then 28 ... ♖c4 keeps Black on top, according to Karpov himself. The key is 29 ♘xg5 fg 30 ♖xg5+ ♔f7 31 ♖f3+ ♔e6 32 ♖ff5, when 32 ... ♖xg4+ demolishes

White's mating net. Still, with 31 ♖f5+ ♔g8 32 ♖g5+ ♗g7 33 ♗d8 ♖xd8 34 ♖e7 White has chances to draw. He will regain one piece and the doubled rooks on the seventh should guard against loss. Nevertheless, this route to equality comes under the heading of "running for the draw", which Karpov was psychologically reluctant to do. Karpov described 28 ♖d5 as a "very bad move", with the accent on the "very".

28	...		♗xd4	96
29	♖xd4	116	♖h8	109
30	♖e1	127	♖c2	111
31	a4	128	a5	111

If 31 ... ♔g6 32 a5 holds.

32 f4! *134*

Karpov called this a "brave" solution, and he was clearly proud of taking such a bold measure when short of time. It is probably the only way to draw. White's passed pawn has become a source of static rather than dynamic strength, and although the position is objectively level, and always has been, it is White who really has to demonstrate equality.

32	...		♔g6	126

33 fg *136*

Karpov later pointed out the fascinating variation 33 f5+ ♔f7 34 ♗xf6 ♘xf6 35 ♖e7+ ♔f8 36 ♖e6 ♘d7 37 ♖e7 drawing since ... ♘c5 fails to f6.

33	...		♔xg5	128
34	♖f1	137	♔g6	130
35	♖f2!	142		

Accuracy to the end. If 35 ♖df4 ♖hh2 36 ♖xf6+ ♘xf6 37 ♖xf6+ ♔g7 38 d7 then 38 ... ♖hg2+ 39 ♔f1 ♖gd2 wins easily for Black.

35	...		♖hc8	130
36	♖df4	143	♖xf2	136

In playing this Kasparov offered a draw which Karpov promptly accepted.

Draw Agreed

Kasparov	½ 0 ½ 1 0 ½ ½ 1 ½ ½ 1 ½ ½	7
Karpov	½ 1 ½ 0 1 ½ ½ 0 ½ ½ 0 ½ ½	6

GAME FOURTEEN, 16 November

After the tantalising tussle on Friday, game 14, Kasparov's third draw in a row as White, came as a severe disappointment.

At the start of play Karpov had arrived over five minutes late and once again Kasparov allowed his clock to run. By the time Karpov arrived on stage the photographers had already been shooed away by the chief arbiter. In a TV interview later, Karpov explained that he had actually arrived at the theatre early but had gone to his recreation room backstage, closed his eyes and lost track of the time (!).

He described the gift he had bestowed on Kasparov in game 11 as "... like a blessing from Heaven – I would certainly hang on to it as Kasparov is doing now. But there is still a long and very intense fight ahead. An advantage of one point is not decisive and cannot guarantee a quiet life." Prescient words.

	Kasparov-Karpov								
	Caro-Kann Defence				11	0-0	23	♗d6	18
					12	♕d3	36	♗c7	20
					13	♗f3	36	♕d7	30
1	e4	00	c6	00	14	♖d1	42	0-0	37
2	d4	00	d5	00	15	c4	55	♖ad8	47
3	♘d2	00	de	00	16	♕b3	70	♕e7	54
4	♘xe4	00	♘d7	00	17	g3	78	♗b8	56
5	♘f3	00	♘gf6	01	18	♗e3	79	♖d7	71
6	♘xf6+	01	♘xf6	01	19	♖d2	85	♖fd8	72
7	c3	01	♗g4	01	20	♖ad1	85	h6	75
8	h3	01	♗xf3	02	21	a3	96	Draw Agreed	
9	♕xf3	01	♕d5	03		If Black does nothing White has			
10	♗e2	01	e6	08		no chance of breaking through.			

Kasparov	½ 0 ½ 1 0 ½ ½ 1 ½ ½ 1 ½ ½ ½	7½
Karpov	½ 1 ½ 0 1 ½ ½ 0 ½ ½ 0 ½ ½ ½	6½

GAME FIFTEEN, 20 November

This game was widely regarded as the best and most exciting in the match so far. First impressions that one or other player might have overlooked a winning continuation were dispelled by closer analysis, showing that both of them handled the complications with pinpoint accuracy.

The loudest action came off the board. When the game was adjourned it was generally expected that a draw would be rapidly agreed and that there would be no further play. But Karpov delayed his offer until noon the next day, a lapse of fifteen hours after the adjournment (chess etiquette requires that the player with a nominal advantage – in this case Karpov – must be the one to offer the draw). When chief arbiter Geurt Gijssen phoned, Kasparov was out; the second time his cook, Catalina, took the call. She said he was asleep and could not be disturbed. By the time Gijssen finally did get through, Karpov himself was seething. The challenger told Gijssen that his original offer had been made only by his driver, Vladimir Pischenko, and was therefore invalid. The invaluable Pischenko, who has a triple role as translator, chauffeur and bodyguard, had often acted for Karpov in the past, and was entirely *persona grata*. Gijssen decided there was no way under the rules that the offer could be withdrawn.

At 4.30 p.m., the hour for play to resume, the Teatro Lope de Vega was alive with expectant spectators. Neither player was on stage, nor was the clock running. Then Karpov came forward, only to be shooed backstage by Gijssen, who formally announced the draw.

Kasparov marched into the press room and accused Karpov of impolite behaviour. "If he can spend fifteen hours deciding to offer the draw, why can't I spend three hours deciding whether to accept?" he demanded. With the world champion in mid-sentence, Gijssen came in with the news that Karpov had now signed the scoresheet. Karpov then arrived to have his say. "Of course the position is drawn. I just wanted to draw attention to the incorrect behaviour of my opponent," he averred.

There was a witty postscript to this small incident. Later that evening Josef Dorfman and Dominic Lawson related the day's events to a newly arrived spectator, who commented that this sounded like the first world championship game where the draw had been offered by a chauffeur and declined by a cook. Noting Lawson's amused reaction, Dorfman said: "My friend, why are you laughing? This is normal situation in world chess championship."

Karpov-Kasparov
Grünfeld Defence

1	d4	00	♘f6	00
2	c4	00	g6	01
3	♘c3	00	d5	01

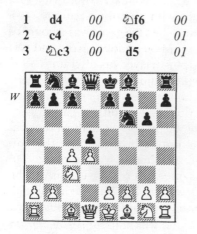

On past occasions we have had some harsh words for Kasparov's Grünfeld Defence. He sticks to it religiously as an antidote to Karpov's 1 d4, yet Kasparov's score with Black is not particularly impressive. He has lost games 5, 17 and 19 from the 1986 match and game 5 here. Along with numerous draws, this is not an attractive proposition.

However, in recent games in Seville the Grünfeld's stock has been rising. Kasparov has been demonstrating theoretical equality for Black in a number of key lines. He actually notched his first Black win (albeit an eleemosynary one) in game 11, and games 13 and 15 have been some of the sharpest and most exciting these two great champions have created.

It is fitting that the outstanding game 15 from Seville was concluded on Grünfeld's birthday, 21 November.

4	♘f3	00	♝g7	01
5	♕b3	00		

Karpov reverts for the first time to the variation which netted him the most points in their previous match. Of course, in the interim Kasparov has been refurbishing his arsenal, but in this game it is Karpov who comes up with the new move.

5	...		dc	02
6	♕xc4	00	0-0	02
7	e4	00	♘a6	04

The Prins Variation, as used in game 19 from Leningrad, a great Karpov triumph.

| 8 | ♝e2 | 01 | c5 | 04 |

75

9	d5	*01*	e6	*05*
10	0-0	*01*	ed	*05*
11	ed	*02*	♗f5	*05*

As usual in Karpov-Kasparov Grünfelds Black has challenged the White centre and as a result the first player has obtained an isolated but passed and potentially dangerous d-pawn.

12	♖d1	*02*

Varying from game 19 at Leningrad, where Karpov had won after 12 ♗f4 ♖e8 13 ♖ad1 ♘e4 14 ♘b5 ♕f6 15 ♗d3 ♘b4 16 ♘c7. Kasparov had meanwhile revealed his improvement in a comparatively unimportant game vs Djandjava, Baku 1987: 15 ... ♖ad8! 16 ♖de1 ♕xb2 17 ♘c7 ♘xc7 18 ♗xc7 ♘d2 and Black was well on top. The latest word on this volatile variation was Belyavsky-Kasparov, Moscow TV Speed Chess 1987: 15 d6!? ♗d7 16 g3 g5 17 ♗e3 h6 18 ♘c7 ♘xc7 19 dc ♗c6 and the game ended in a draw. Forewarned of Kasparov's new ideas, Karpov gets his own innovation in first.

12	...	♖e8	*33*
13	d6	*06*	

A very ambitious thrust, reminiscent of game 13 and indeed of earlier Grünfelds (e.g. game 5 at London 1986) between these two players where Karpov established a passed pawn at d6. Of course, White has to make sacrifices to achieve this advance, especially in terms of conceding Black a lead in development based on harassment of the exposed white queen.

13	...	h6!!	*56*

Kasparov invested 23 minutes on this, which denies White access to the g5 square for either his queen's bishop or king's knight. It looks strange to play a semi-waiting move in such a volatile situation, but this clearly ejected Karpov from his prepared analysis and forced him to think – for 29 minutes. White's next prepares a haven for his queen's bishop on h2

76

so that it can stay in touch with the d6 pawn should Black ever play ... ♘h5.

| 14 | h3 | 35 | ♘b4 | 75 |
| 15 | ♗f4 | 71 | | |

The position has now become horrifically complicated. Here, for example, it is too dangerous to play 15 ♕xc5 ♘c2 16 ♖b1 ♘d7, with terrible threats against the discoordinated White forces.

| 15 | ... | | ♘d7 | 77 |
| 16 | ♖d2!! | 77 | | |

A Roland for Black's Oliver. This move is the introduction to a splendid and deeply conceived regrouping manoeuvre. White's queen is chased ignominiously back to base, but the important thing is that the d6 pawn survives in all its glory.

| 16 | ... | | a6 | 80 |

Preparing pawn expansion with a vengeance. For a while to come Black appears to be dictating events.

| 17 | ♕b3 | 79 | b5 | 84 |

| 18 | ♕d1 | 87 | c4 | 90 |
| 19 | a4 | 102 | ♘c5 | 93 |

Taimanov, the distinguished Soviet grandmaster and commentator, criticised this move as premature, recommending instead 19 ... ♖b8. In that case, however, White can gain distinct counterchances with 20 ab ab 21 ♖a7 ♕b6 22 ♖c7.

| 20 | ab | 106 | ♘bd3 | 102 |

If 20 ... ♘b3 21 ♖a4 ♘xd2 22 ♖xb4 ♘e4 23 ♘d5 ♘xd6 24 b6 and White has the initiative.

Black's initiative reaches its climax. It is curious how themes seem to recur in games between these players. This position, for example, calls to mind strongly game 16 of their 1985 match (Karpov White) and game 16 of their match last year (Kasparov White). Common features are a white passed pawn on d6 and a black knight penetrating to the d3 square.

| 21 | ♗xd3 | 114 | ♘xd3 | 102 |
| 22 | ♖xd3 | 115 | | |

This exchange sacrifice is obligatory. If White's bishop on f4 moves Black will win with ... ♘xb2.

| 22 | ... | cd | 107 |

This is probably over-ambitious. Black should play 22 ... ♗xd3, when 23 ♖xa6 is OK for White. The position would be in dynamic equilibrium.

| 23 | ♘d5 | 117 |

The start of a tremendous counterattack which brings Karpov to the verge of victory.

| 23 | ... | ab | 111 |
| 24 | ♘e7+ | 122 |

This is much stronger than 24 ♖xa8 ♕xa8 25 ♘c7, when White regains the exchange but faces a highly dubious endgame. This way White eliminates the black passed pawn whilst retaining his own.

24	...	♔h7	113
25	♖xa8	123	♕xa8	113
26	♘xf5	123	gf	114
27	♕xd3	123	♕e4	123
28	♕xb5	125	♖a8	126

Karpov has great compensation for the lost exchange and it is now Black who is struggling for the draw. Note that Black could not capture White's bishop on f4 since his rook is en prise to the white queen.

| 29 | ♗d2 | 128 |

Rightly avoiding 29 ♗g3? f4 30 ♗h4 ♖a1+ 31 ♔h2 ♕b1 with a mating attack.

| 29 | ... | ♖d8 | 126 |
| 30 | ♕c5 | 131 |

It is still too early to be sure, but preliminary analysis indicates that White would have come closer to victory with 30 ♕b6, defending b2.

30	...	♕e6	136
31	♗f4	132	♗xb2	137
32	♘h4	134	♗f6	138

| 33 | ♕xf5+ | 140 |

Taking with the queen leads to a clearly drawn ending where Black can always sacrifice his rook for White's passed d-pawn and knight.

If, however, 33 ♘xf5 then 33 ... ♖c8 34 ♕b5 ♕e1+ 35 ♔h2 ♕xf2

78

36 ♗e3 is very unclear, while 34 ♕a5 ♗d8 35 ♕b5 ♕e1+ leads to similar variations. In the mutual time scramble to reach move 40 Karpov obviously did not want to take any chances.

33	...		♕xf5	139
34	♘xf5	140	h5	139
35	g4	143	hg	139
36	hg	143	♔g6	139
37	♔g2	144	♗b2	139
38	♘e7+	144	♔f6	140
39	♘c6	146	♖d7	140
40	♘b8	146	♖d8	142
41	d7	147	♔e6	142

Now White could play 42 ♗c7, but 42 ... ♖xd7 43 ♘xd7 ♔xd7 is an absolutely dead draw. The extra pawn in such positions is meaningless.

42 ♔f3 *149* ♗a3 *144*

Somewhat surprisingly, instead of agreeing a draw Karpov now sealed his 43rd move.

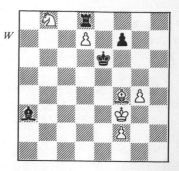

43 ♗c7 *155* **Draw Agreed**

Kasparov	½	0	½	1	0	½	½	1	½	½	1	½	½	½	½	8
Karpov	½	1	½	0	1	½	½	0	½	½	0	½	½	½	½	7

GAME SIXTEEN, 23 November

After lying doggo with White in games 10, 12 and 14, Kasparov leapt out and made a vigorous effort to win game 16 and prove that White really does start with the initiative. But he lost and Karpov equalised the match at 8-8.

Various explanations were offered to explain Kasparov's downfall. The fact is that Karpov, after producing some crisp opening play, fended off Kasparov's over-ambitious middlegame attack with superb accuracy. He never really gave his opponent a chance. Along with game 2 (which it strangely resembled), game 16 was Karpov's best performance of the match so far.

Karpov gave an interesting interview to Spanish TV after this game:
Leontxo García: Some people say that this game was lost by Kasparov, others that you won it. What is your opinion?
Karpov: During the last matches I have got used to the fact that the journalists describe our games in a monotonous way. Kasparov loses, Kasparov wins. And Karpov simply attends at the games, unfortunately not always in the best possible way. The last game was very interesting. In the beginning Kasparov had the initiative. I managed to defend quite successfully, in an active way. When Kasparov understood that his initiative was crumbling, he decided to continue by complicating the game instead of suffering a difficult ending. He found no chance in these complications and resigned.
Leontxo García: Theoretically the score is still favourable for Kasparov because he retains the title in the event of a tied match. However, your psychological advantage seems more important.
Karpov: Of course, Kasparov has still an advantage of one point, though the score is now level. From a psychological point of view, I am now in a better situation since I managed to equalise the score. But this psychological advantage comes and goes. I had had an advantage of one point, which is more important than the odds of the draw, and therefore the real fight is still ahead.

Kasparov-Karpov
English Opening

Karpov arrived a full five minutes late for the start of the game and, as usual, Kasparov did not make his first move until his opponent was in place.

1 c4 00

Clearly sick of short draws against the Caro-Kann, Kasparov switches back to the English.

1	...	e5	01
2	♘c3	00	♘f6	01
3	♘f3	00	♘c6	01
4	g3	00	♗b4	01
5	♗g2	01	0-0	02
6	0-0	01	♖e8	04

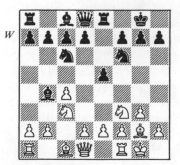

The first deviation from games 2 and 4, where Karpov had advanced ... e4 before playing ... ♖e8. His new move order is more flexible.

7 d3 03

7 ♘d5 is generally considered to be a more testing move, e.g. 7 ... ♘xd5 8 cd ♘d4 9 ♘e1 c6 10 e3 ♘b5 11 d3 and White has the edge,

Petrosian-Kuzmin, USSR Ch 1974.

7	...	♗xc3	06
8	bc	03	e4	06
9	♘d4	03		

If 9 ♘g5 then 9 ... ed 10 ed h6 transposes to a harmless variation from games 2 and 4 where White is committed to d3 instead of f3.

9 ... h6 07

After 9 ... ed 10 ed ♘xd4 11 cd d5 12 ♗e3 the opening favoured White in Botvinnik-Basman, Hastings 1966-67, though in fact the former world champion later had to struggle to draw.

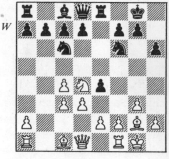

10 de 06

This is the sort of move which wrecks White's pawn structure and which an intelligent pupil would be chastised for playing. When the world champion indulges in this kind of move there has to be a deeper point to it.

10 c5 led to an unbalanced position in Stean-Hartston, British Ch 1972, after 10 ... ed 11 ♕xd3 ♘e5 12 ♕c2 ♕e7 13 ♗a3 ♘c4 14 ♕a4 ♘xa3 15 ♕xa3 ♕e5.

10	...		♘xe4	07
11	♕c2	10	d5	08

Now Kasparov had a very long think and came up with a continuation that is not particularly incisive. He should have played the more vigorous 12 ♖d1!, e.g. 12 ... ♘xd4 13 ♖xd4 ♕f6 14 e3 ♗f5 15 f3 ♘xg3 16 ♕b2 ♘h5 17 cd followed by e4, when White's bishops and centre pawns should give him the edge. This is a line worked out by the Norwegian grandmaster Simen Agdestein, part professional footballer, part professional chessplayer, who is one of the leading lights of the analysis room.

12	cd	46	♕xd5	09

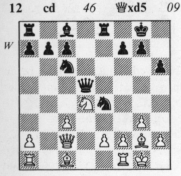

13	e3	62

Kasparov was still consuming tremendous amounts of time over his moves. Here is an example of the tricky forcing variations contained in this position: 13 ♖d1 ♗f5 14 ♘xf5 (14 f3 ♘f2!! 15 e4 ♘xd1 16 ♕xd1 ♕c5 17 ef ♕xc3 and Black wins) 14 ... ♕xf5 15 ♗e3 ♘xg3 16 ♕b2 ♘e4 17 ♕xb7 ♘a5!

18 ♖d5 (18 ♕xc7 ♖ac8 19 ♕xa7 ♘xc3 gives Black excellent play) 18 ... ♕xf2+ 19 ♗xf2 ♘xb7 20 ♖d7 ♖ac8! 21 ♗xa7 ♘bd6 with the embarrassing threat of ... ♘f6.

13	...		♘a5	47

The black knight begins to home in on the weak c4 square.

14	f3	86	♘d6	53
15	e4	86	♕c5	55

As Kasparov played his next move he accidentally knocked over his king. A portent?

16	♗e3	93	♘dc4	64
17	♗f2	94	♕e7	64

In the press room Tal favoured 17 ... ♕a3, but it looked premature. His fellow kibitzers were able to exploit the queen's absence to develop strong kingside pressure.

18	♖ad1	100	♗d7	77

There is now some order in the White camp and even prospects of aggression by means of a central advance to free his bishop pair. Kasparov's problem is that after mobilising his forces Black will have positional threats of his own, such as the above-mentioned ... ♕a3, plus ... ♗a4 and ... c5, driving away White's well posted knight. With less than an hour on his clock and perhaps concerned at Black's future activity, Kasparov now decides to launch an all-out attack of his own. This was brave but perhaps not wise.

| 19 | f4 | 103 | ♖ad8 | 85 |
| 20 | e5 | 106 | ♗g4! | 99 |

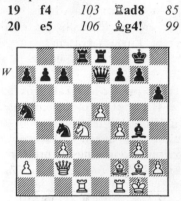

A very fine intermediary move which disturbs the flow of White's plans.

21	♘f5	108	♕e6	104
22	♖xd8	108	♖xd8	104
23	♘d4	109	♕c8!	106

A further fine move and exactly the right place for the black queen. The main point is to keep control over the c8-h3 diagonal.

This super-accurate retreat was totally overlooked by the gang of GMs in the press room. Tal, Gufeld and Polugayevsky had considered only 23 ... ♕e8, when White has

24 h3 and 25 ♖e1 with a threatening kingside initiative – the knight will drop back to f3 after ... c5 to cover the d2 square.

| 24 | f5 | 118 |

If 24 ♗e4 c5 25 ♗f5 ♗xf5 26 ♘xf5 is strong, but 24 ... ♕d7 keeps Black on top.

| 24 | ... | c5 | 113 |

| 25 | ♕e4 | 119 |

25 h3 cd 26 ♗xd4!? may be an improvement here. If Black tries 26 ... ♘d2 White has 27 ♖f4!, with the following variations:

a) 27 ... ♖xd4?! 28 ♖xd4 ♘f3+ 29 ♗xf3 ♗xf3 30 ♕d3 ♘c6 (30 ... ♕c6 31 e6 is very strong) 31 ♕xf3 ♘xd4 32 cd and White is a pawn up.

b) 27 ... ♘f3+ 28 ♗xf3 ♗xf3 29 ♕a4 ♘c6 (29 ... ♖xd4 30 ♕xd4 looks dangerous for Black) 30 ♖xf3 ♘xd4 31 cd ♕c1+ 32 ♔g2 ♕d2+ 33 ♖f2 with equality.

The situation is now terribly complicated and most players would have blown up when faced by Kasparov's attacking genius.

Instead, Karpov's mental machete cuts right through the complexities and strikes directly at the weak point of Kasparov's bold combination.

| 25 | ... | cd | *118* |

Not 25 ... ♘d2 26 ♕xg4 ♘xf1 27 e6 cd 28 f6 g6 29 ef+ ♔xf7 30 ♗d5+ ♔f8 31 ♕xg6 and White wins. But another possibility for Black, strongly tipped in the press room, is 25 ... h5, maintaining the tension. The solution chosen by Karpov, however, is the neatest.

| 26 | ♕xg4 | *127* |

| 26 | ... | ♘xe5 | *133* |

The crux of Black's cunning defence. Karpov avoids 26 ... dc 27 e6, which is not at all clear. If now 27 ♕e4 (which is the natural reply) then 27 ... ♘ec4 28 ♗xd4 ♘d2 29 ♕e5 ♖xd4 30 cd ♘xf1 31 ♗xf1 ♘c6 and however White continues he suffers from lack of co-ordination in the queen and knight versus queen and bishop endgame, not least because his king is inadequately protected.

| 27 | ♕e2 | *122* | ♘ec6 | *135* |
| 28 | cd | *125* | ♘xd4 | *135* |

| 29 | ♗xd4? | *126* |

This is the losing move. Kasparov clearly did not want to waste time but he overlooked Black's strong 30th move. White must simply move his queen here, perhaps to b2 as advocated by the Swedish grandmaster Ulf Andersson. In that case White would stand objectively worse but there would be chances for obfuscation in mutual time trouble.

| 29 | ... | ♖xd4 | *135* |
| 30 | f6 | *126* | ♕e6 | *138* |

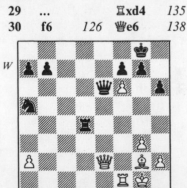

This decides the game. White can hardly afford to trade queens since he is a pawn in arrears and meanwhile the apparently scattered Black forces assume dominant posts in the centre of the board – the key battlefield, as every strategist knows. What follows is agony for Kasparov.

31	♕b2	*140*	♕e3+	*138*
32	♔h1	*140*	b6	*140*
33	fg	*140*	♘c4	*140*
34	♕c2	*141*	♔xg7	*142*
35	♗d5	*144*	♘d6	*146*

Of course Black refuses to complicate his technical task by taking White's useless bishop.

| 36 | ♕h2 | *145* | ♕e5 | *147* |
| 37 | ♗b3 | *146* | a5 | *148* |

38	♕f2	*146*	f5	*148*
39	♕b2	*147*	b5	*148*
40	a3	*147*	♔g6	*149*

Kasparov now sealed **41** ♕f2 (*167*) but resigned without wishing to be shown the proof of Karpov's superiority.

White Resigns

| Kasparov | ½ 0 ½ 1 0 ½ ½ 1 ½ ½ 1 ½ ½ ½ ½ 0 | 8 |
| Karpov | ½ 1 ½ 0 1 ½ ½ 0 ½ ½ 0 ½ ½ ½ ½ 1 | 8 |

GAME SEVENTEEN, 25 November

Karpov surprised us all by abandoning his favourite 1 d4 and playing the less aggressive 1 ♘f3. Does this mean that he has finally given up against the Grünfeld? Kasparov then hit us with a second surprise – he chose to defend with the King's Indian, a risky counterattacking defence which does not enjoy a high reputation at this exalted level. Indeed, one cannot recall another main line King's Indian in a world title match since Spassky lost on the Black side to Petrosian in game 12 of the 1966 championship.

Whatever the theoretical merits or demerits of the Black defence, Karpov was clearly unfamiliar with it and pondered hard in the opening stages. In fact he ended up mislaying a whole tempo on a main line, but a characteristically subtle interpretation of the middlegame still left White dictating the course of events. Karpov's 17th move was widely praised, while in contrast nobody could really comprehend Kasparov's over-refined bishop thrust on move 18.

White's pressure gradually evaporated after a series of exchanges but towards the close of the session Kasparov missed an easy draw in the rook and pawn ending. Still, at adjournment the entire grandmaster corps, including such luminaries as Mark Taimanov, Eddie 'Caviar' Gufeld, Lev Polugayevsky and 'Mr Endgames' himself, Yuri Averbakh, all expected a short and painless draw. But appearances can be as deceptive in chess as anywhere else. Although the position was indeed ultimately a draw, it contained variations of enormous complexity (which even Karpov missed in his overnight analysis) and would have required very accurate play from the champion. Kasparov in fact only stumbled on these possibilities an hour before resumption, and analysed frantically until the last minute. He arrived at the board an unprecedented fifteen minutes late and appeared flustered when play began. However, once the draw had been signed he broke into a broad grin and proceeded to demonstrate key variations from his analysis to his opponent. This friendly conclusion to the game was the first time the two had analysed together in Seville and made a pleasing contrast with the bickering over retracted draw offers which had marred the conclusion of game 15.

Karpov-Kasparov
King's Indian Defence

Before this game Yeganov, Kasparov's head of delegation, was asked how the champion felt about his defeat the previous day. He replied philosophically: "Victory and defeat are brothers in sport" – from which it can be presumed that Kasparov was not tearing his hair out over the loss.

| 1 | ♘f3 | 00 |
| | | |

Finally Karpov varies from 1 d4.

1	...	♘f6	07
2	c4	00	g6	08
3	♘c3	01	♗g7	09

Kasparov indicates that he is willing to enter the King's Indian. The alternative, of course, would have been ... d5 at once, which might transpose to a main line Grünfeld, but White has other tries, such as 4 cd ♘xd5 5 ♕a4+. The King's Indian used to be one of Kasparov's favourites, but he gave it up after close shaves against Timman, who used the Sämisch Variation. The Sämisch (with f3 for White) is no longer an option here, and the King's Indian has the additional attraction that Karpov is not exactly an expert on the White side of this opening.

4	e4	03	d6	09
5	d4	05	0-0	09
6	♗e2	07	e5	09
7	0-0	07	♘c6	09
8	d5	19	♘e7	09
9	♘d2	19		

Just one of a myriad possibilities – 9 b4, 9 ♘e1, 9 ♗d2 etc.

| 9 | ... | a5 | 09 |
| 10 | b3 | 21 | | |

A curious move which loses a tempo. Normal would be 10 ♖b1 followed by a3 and b4, saving a whole move over the game continuation.

| 10 | ... | c5 | 13 |
| 11 | a3 | 27 | ♘e8 | 15 |

Kasparov prepares the traditional counteraction with ... f5.

12	♖b1	28	f5	15
13	b4	28	ab	15
14	ab	28	b6	15
15	♕b3	37	♘f6	32

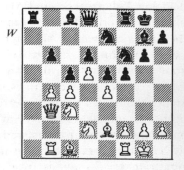

Compare the opening here with Taimanov-Kavalek, Wijk aan Zee 1970. There the same position arose but with Black not having the move ... ♘f6. That game continued 15 bc bc 16 ♕b6 ♘f6 17 ♕xd8 ♖xd8 18 f3 ♗h6 with equality. In theory, therefore, since Black now has an extra tempo he should experience no problems at all in this instance.

16 ♗d3 45

Karpov has to proceed somewhat defensively, at first fortifying the e4 pawn. Having forfeited an entire tempo he does not have time to continue as Taimanov did with bc and ♕b6.

16 ... ♗h6 41

An excellent and active diagonal for Black's King's Indian bishop.

17 ♖b2 55

An absolutely typical Karpov move, quietly improving the position of his pieces, strengthening his inner lines of communication and refusing to undertake any hasty action. This kind of move also tends to have the effect of waving a red rag in front of a bull when played against Kasparov. The world champion now launches, after profound thought, a violent invasion of White's camp, but the best course would have been the simple 17 ... ♘h5, and if 18 g3 (creating a weakness) then 18 ... ♘f6 with full equality, as one would expect.

17 ... ♖a1 84

The main merit of this move is that White cannot co-ordinate sufficiently to surround the intrusive rook.

18 ♕c2 77 ♗f4 94

What a strange idea. Some GMs in the press room were advocating 18 ... ♗xd2 and ... f4, but it cannot be correct to give up the valuable king's bishop in this carefree fashion. Once again, 18 ... ♘h5 looks natural.

19 ♘f3 88

A fine restrained riposte which leads by force to the exchange of all of Black's adventurously placed pieces.

Naturally, Karpov is not interested in voluntarily weakening his position with 19 g3.

19	...		fe	106
20	♘xe4	88	♘xe4	106
21	♗xe4	88	♖xc1	109
22	♖xc1	90	♗xc1	109
23	♕xc1	90	♘f5	110

24 ♕g5 *110*

At first sight a 'wimpish' solution to the problems of the position since White appears to have an incipient initiative on the a- and b-files, and the exchange of queens removes some momentum from this. On deeper inspection, though, Black's counterplay based on ... ♘d4 will be less effective in the endgame.

24 ... ♘d4 *124*

Ensuring further simplification and a drawish conclusion.

25	♕xd8	*111*	♘xf3+	*124*
26	♗xf3	*111*	♖xd8	*124*
27	bc	*111*	bc	*124*
28	♖b8	*111*	♖f8	*124*

The only way to unpin, but good enough.

29	♖b6	*111*	♖f6	*129*
30	♖b8	*132*	♖f8	*129*
31	♖b6	*132*	♖f6	*129*
32	♗e4	*139*		

Karpov decides to continue, though objectively he still has nothing.

32	...		♗f5	*130*
33	♗xf5	*139*	♖xf5!	*130*

This accurate reply should really have forced a draw in short order, while 33 ... gf 34 f3 would permit White to plough on with a tiny edge.

34 g3 *140*

If 34 ♖xd6 ♖f4 35 ♖e6 ♖xc4 36 g3 ♖d4 37 ♖xe5 c4 with an immediate and obvious draw.

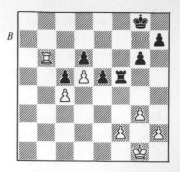

B

34 ... ♖f6? *132*

It is strange that Kasparov now misses an identical drawing device. He could have avoided much future toil and sweat by playing 34 ... ♖f3 and ... ♖c3 which draws in exactly the same way as in the previous note, even though Black is a tempo down. Perhaps that would have been the revenge for the tempo White lost in the opening.

35	h4	*141*	h6	*134*
36	♔g2	*141*	♔g7	*135*
37	f3	*142*	♔g8	*134*
38	♔f2	*144*	g5	*139*
39	hg	*145*	hg	*139*
40	♔e3	*145*	♔g7	*140*
41	♖b8	*149*	♔h7	*141*

Black has an important defensive resource in this ending, which has suddenly become difficult after the earlier easy draw by 34 ... ♖f3 was missed. The resource is based on ... g4 at the right moment. This thrust either liquidates completely (if White responds f4) or leads to a totally unwinnable endgame for

White if he captures on g4. Nevertheless, this is emphatically not the right moment. If 41 ... g4 42 f4 ef+ 43 gf g3 44 ﬅb2 and the rook stops and wins Black's g-pawn. The ... g4 resource only functions when White's rook is absent from the a- or b-files and therefore cannot get back sufficiently quickly to impede the g-pawn.

42   ﬅd8   *155*   ♚g7?   *146*

Black's sealed move – it is much too carefree and deserves its '?'. Here 42 ... g4 would actually draw. After 43 fg the extra pawn is worthless and White will never be able to gain anything by going into a king and pawn ending since Black has a protected passed e-pawn. Alternatively, 42 ... g4 43 f4 ef+ 44 gf g3 45 ﬅa8 g2 46 ﬅa1 ﬅg6 47 ﬅg1 ♚h6 48 ♚f3 ♚h5 with a draw.

43   ﬅa8   *156*

This throws away the chance to play the line that Kasparov greatly feared and which he had discovered just before play resumed.

Karpov now has the God-given, one might almost say accidental, chance to make life really tough for Black. The point is that now and now only White can get his rook to d7 with check while his king is still on e3. Having played his rook to a8 White can never re-create this fortunate concatenation of circumstances since Black can always arrange to meet ﬅd7 with ... g4. White cannot play g4 first himself as that allows ... ﬅf4.

Having discussed the position in principle the variation follows that whizzed past on the computer screens as Kasparov and Karpov analysed together after the game. Kasparov in an interview said he could not control himself and just had to find out what Karpov had seen in his overnight analysis. It seems that the whole idea had been quite overlooked by the Karpov team as, indeed, it almost was by Kasparov's merry men. The main line is: 43 ﬅd7+ ♚g6 44 g4 ♚h6 45 ♚d2. White's plan is to run his king around the queen's flank: ♚c2-b3-a4-b5 etc. While doing this White tries to save his pawn on c4, which defends d5 and is therefore considerably more important than the pawn on f3. Black's task is somehow to get the pawn on c4. So . . . 45 ... ﬅf4 46 ﬅxd6+ ♚g7 47 ♚d3 ﬅxf3+ 48 ♚e4 ﬅf4+ 49 ♚xe5 ﬅxg4 50 ﬅc6 ﬅxc4 51 d6 ♚f7 52 ﬅc7+

♔e8 53 ♔d5 and now the final difficult move, 53 ... ♖a4 – to meet 54 ♔c6 with 54 ... ♖a6+. This is the study-like draw to which Kasparov referred in his interview after the game. No wonder, having missed this overnight, the champion arrived fifteen minutes late for the session and looked unshaven and haggard.

43	...		♔f7	160
44	♔e4?	157	♔g7	160
45	♖a7+	163	♔g6	161
46	♖e7	178	g4!	

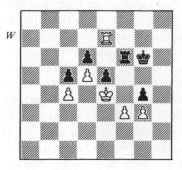

Draw Agreed

On Karpov's proposal.

47 gf ♔g5 48 ♖g7+ ♖g6 is drawn as outlined above, while 47 f4 ef 48 gf g3 49 ♔f3 g2 or 49 ♖a7 g2 50 ♖a1 ♔h5 51 ♔f3 ♖g6 52 ♖g1 ♔h4 is also fine.

Black could not draw by playing possum on move 46 with 46 ... ♔h6 on account of an interesting and forced queen endgame: 47 ♖e6 ♔g6 48 ♖xf6+ ♔xf6 49 g4 ♔g6 50 ♔d3 ♔f6 51 ♔c3 e4 52 fe ♔e5 53 ♔b3 ♔xe4 (53 ... ♔d4 54 e5) 54 ♔a4 ♔d3 55 ♔b5 ♔d4 56 ♔c6 ♔xc4 57 ♔xd6 ♔b4 58 ♔e6 c4 59 d6 c3 60 d7 c2 61 d8♕ c1♕ 62 ♕b6+ and ♔f5 with a probable win in practice if not in theory, since the black g-pawn will ultimately fall. This ending could also have arisen if Black had mistakenly put his king on the back rank in response to possible rook checks on the 7th rank, e.g. on move 41 had White played ♖b7+.

Kasparov	½	0	½	1	0	½	½	1	½	½	1	½	½	½	½	0	½	**8½**
Karpov	½	1	½	0	1	½	½	0	½	½	0	½	½	½	½	1	½	**8½**

GAME EIGHTEEN, 30 November

For the first time since game 8 Kasparov succeeded in putting on real pressure with the white pieces. It will be remembered that games 10, 12 and 14 had been pusillanimous draws for the world champion, while playing White in game 16 Kasparov had gone down in flames. This lack of action with White forms a stark contrast to Kasparov's usually impressive form when the advantage of the first move is allied to his naturally great flair for the initiative.

The opening, the first Tartakower Queen's Gambit of the match, started by duplicating many earlier games between the two. It seemed that Kasparov wanted to mount insidious pressure while avoiding any risk of loss. Nevertheless, White's advantage steadily grew until on move 23 Kasparov chose a too direct continuation of his attack. Karpov swiftly and accurately repelled boarders and transposed into a slightly inferior but drawn rook and pawn ending.

Kasparov was angry with himself after the game. He clearly felt he had missed something substantial and Leontxo García, the Spanish TV interviewer, feared that Kasparov might even storm out of his nightly chat for Spanish viewers. Fortunately Kasparov calmed down.

The commentary for the game today was conducted by the amusing double act of golden oldies Korchnoi (Soviet defector) and Tal (Soviet ex-world champion). They made a splendid pair, furiously analysing together on the giant hand-operated demonstration board in the theatre foyer. Sadly Tal had to leave Seville soon afterwards, and the ubiquitous Leontxo, now writing as correspondent of *El País*, came right out and accused Karpov of having engineered his departure. Tal had, indeed, once been Karpov's second and now he is known to be a Kasparov man, so Karpov may possibly have felt uneasy about his presence. Still, it was distressing to see such a famous old warrior of the chessboard have to depart the scene of action when he quite obviously wanted to stay on. This was a case where *glasnost* didn't quite make it to the finishing line.

Kasparov-Karpov
Queen's Gambit Declined

| 1 | c4 | 00 |
| | | |

Karpov is habitually late and hitherto Kasparov has waited until his opponent arrives before making his first move. Today for the first time Kasparov did not wait. Karpov duly turned up two minutes late to find his clock already running.

| 1 | ... | e6 | 02 |

Karpov does not repeat his "dubious experiment", as Kasparov dubbed his handling of the opening in game 16.

2	♘c3	00	d5	02
3	d4	01	♗e7	02
4	♘f3	05		

Saving the sharper 4 cd for a rainy day.

4	...	♘f6	03
5	♗g5	05	h6	07
6	♗h4	06		

A slight surprise, since both players have in the most recent games tortured each other with 6 ♗xf6. It turns out that Kasparov has a specific variation in mind, also very popular in earlier K-K games, where White maintains a very slight edge with absolutely no risk of loss.

6	...	0-0	08
7	e3	06	b6	09
8	♗e2	07	♗b7	14
9	♗xf6	07	♗xf6	14
10	cd	07	ed	16

11	b4	07	c5	21
12	bc	08	bc	21
13	♖b1	08	♗c6	24
14	0-0	08	♘d7	25
15	♗b5	08	♕c7	25
16	♕d3	08		

This position is not new, in fact the last occasion on which it was seen at summit level was in game 8 of the 1985 match (Karpov White). Now Karpov sank into thought for 42 minutes and then varied from Kasparov's choice, which had been 16 ... ♖fd8. Opening fortune in the two Ks' games with this line (see also games 12, 38, 39, 40 and 42 of their first match) has fluctuated between a clear advantage to White and dead equality, but all the games have ended as draws.

16	...	♖fc8	67
17	♖fc1	15	♖ab8	72
18	h3	30	g6	81
19	♗xc6	71	♖xb1	86
20	♕xb1	72	♕xc6	87
21	dc	72	♕xc5	94

Hereabouts Kasparov asked the arbiter to adjust his small heater on the stage. Both players have their own little electic fire to minimise cold from draughts etc.

| 22 | ♘e2 | *74* | ♕f8 | *95* |

Kasparov invested a tremendous amount of energy in his next, aggressive-seeming move, but he had underestimated Karpov's reply which forces simplification adequate to hold the draw. The correct line is 23 ♘f4 tying Black to the defence of the d5 pawn, and only then h4, seeking to break open Black's king's wing with h5. It was probably the omission of ♘f4 that made Kasparov so furious with himself at the end of the game.

| 23 | h4? | *106* | ♘e5! | *114* |

One could now predict that the game would have to end in a draw.

| 24 | ♘xe5 | *101* | ♗xe5 | *116* |
| 25 | ♖d1 | *105* | ♕c5 | *118* |

| 26 | h5 | *109* | ♕c2! | *123* |

A perfect response to all White's threats. Although Kasparov retains an infinitesimal edge in the rook and pawn endgame it is nowhere near enough to cause Karpov serious trouble.

27	♕xc2	*111*	♖xc2	*123*
28	♖xd5	*111*	♖xe2	*124*
29	♖xe5	*111*	♖xa2	*124*
30	hg	*111*	fg	*124*
31	♖e7	*111*	a5	*128*
32	♖a7	*112*	a4	*129*
33	g3	*125*	h5	*139*

White's only chance is to activate his king and push the e-pawn, but Karpov swiftly quashes this danger.

| 34 | ♔g2 | *117* | a3 | *139* |
| 35 | e4 | *119* | g5! | *141* |

If now 36 ♖a5 g4 37 ♖xh5 ♖e2, and Black's active rook and passed pawn combine to prevent White's king from ever escaping into the open.

36	♔f3	*124*	g4+	*146*
37	♔e3	*124*	♖a1	*147*
38	♔f4	*125*		

White must actually be careful here. After the incautious 38 e5 a2 39 ♔f4 h4 40 gh g3 it is White who is in trouble.

38	...		♖f1	*147*
39	♔g5	*131*	♖xf2	*147*
40	♔xh5	*131*	♖e2	*147*

Draw Agreed

| Kasparov | ½ | 0 | ½ | 1 | 0 | ½ | ½ | 1 | ½ | ½ | 1 | ½ | ½ | ½ | ½ | 0 | ½ | ½ | **9** |
| Karpov | ½ | 1 | ½ | 0 | 1 | ½ | ½ | 0 | ½ | ½ | 0 | ½ | ½ | ½ | ½ | 1 | ½ | ½ | **9** |

GAME NINETEEN, 2 December

Karpov again avoided the Grünfeld by sticking to his new love 1 ♘f3, but Kasparov gave us all a shock by unhesitatingly opting for the very defence (Queen's Gambit Tartakower) with which Karpov himself had suffered in the previous game. Vasily Smyslov, the Olympian former world champion, commented: "Why do they play this stupid line? Black has no counterplay at all."

Indeed, so it proved. Karpov, not satisfied with the small plus which Kasparov had achieved in game 18, produced a significant improvement. From then on (as Jon Tisdall neatly put it) Kasparov had to relearn the discipline of suffering which he had tasted so bitterly in the long defensive battles of the first super-K match back in 1984-5.

For a period Black's position looked critical – the set-ups were almost symmetrical but White had a clear initiative and Black's remaining bishop looked a mere spectator. Then, however, Kasparov revealed what a great player he is under pressure. First he sacrificed a pawn to liberate his bishop, and when Karpov sidestepped middlegame complications to transpose to an ending with an extra pawn (passed on the a-file) Kasparov kept White at bay with remarkably accurate and ingenious defence.

At adjournment nobody truly believed that Karpov had winning chances any more. Tal (by phone from Madrid, en route back to sunny Moscow) said "80 per cent draw", while Korchnoi (still in Seville) broadly concurred.

The prophets were right about the result but not the way it would be achieved. In the second session Kasparov confounded the assembled grandmasters by setting a profound trap into which Karpov promptly fell. Kasparov's 48th move initiated a sequence which offered his g7 pawn as bait. Karpov should have avoided this line but snatched the pawn and ran into a barrage of Kasparov analysis fired off at lightning speed. The key to Black's defence was the ingenious move 57 ... ♔e5, which had eminent grandmasters here such as Smyslov and Gufeld gasping

"Impossible!". It looked as if Karpov could then win easily but deeper inspection revealed that White had absolutely no advantageous continuation.

When Karpov finally acquiesced in a draw there was a repeat performance of the close of game 17 – the two great players sat together for around seven minutes analysing what might have been. Such amicable behaviour between world title matadors is almost unheard of but has become almost a habit in Seville.

The score after nineteen games is now the same as after nineteen games last year.

Meanwhile, off stage, Professor Nathan Divinsky, the Canadian representative at the FIDE Congress, has been making his presence felt. A main opponent of the initial measure to ban Spanish international master Calvo for five years for attacking FIDE in the Dutch magazine *New in Chess*, he is now enjoying new status in the liberal Spanish press for having spoken out against the concept of "thought crime".

The Canadian professor (and Einstein look-alike) has also recently concluded a monster calculation, collating results of all top-level games over the past century on a University of British Columbia computer. His objective was to discover the best players of all time on a mathematical/statistical basis. The answer, causing much controversy here, is that Kasparov emerges as the strongest player of all time, followed closely by Karpov (this makes Seville the strongest match of all time), then Fischer, Botvinnik, Capablanca, Lasker and Korchnoi in that order.

Karpov-Kasparov
Queen's Gambit Declined

| 1 | ♘f3 | 00 |

Still postponing resumption of the Grünfeld debate.

| 1 | ... | d5 | 00 |

Also something of a surprise. This indicates that Kasparov does not want to repeat the King's Indian against a prepared Karpov, nor does he wish to enter a pseudo-Grünfeld line where White is not committed to d4.

| 2 | d4 | 01 | ♘f6 | 03 |
| 3 | c4 | 01 | e6 | 03 |

The old faithful, the Queen's Gambit Declined, seen so often in games between the two, and a reliable standby when other defences look that little bit too risky.

4	♘c3	02	♗e7	04
5	♗g5	06	0-0	04
6	e3	08	h6	04
7	♗h4	08	b6	06
8	♗e2	09	♗b7	07

96

9	♗xf6	10	♗xf6	08
10	cd	10	ed	08
11	0-0	10		

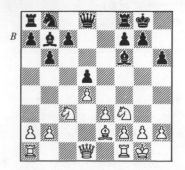

An almost imperceptible deviation from game 18 where Kasparov had White, but this move order does contain more than a drop of poison.

11	...	♘d7	09

Kasparov continues as if nothing worse than transposition to game 18 is in the air.

11 ... c5 is also dubious after 12 dc ♗xc3 (or 12 ... bc 13 ♕b3!) 13 bc bc 14 ♖b1, Kasparov-Torre, Moscow 1981. Theory recommends 11 ... ♕e7 inhibiting b4, but even then White can gain an edge by 12 ♕b3 planning ♖ad1, ♖fe1 and ultimately a central break with e4.

12	b4	13	c5	09
13	bc	13	bc	10
14	♕b3!	14		

An important innovation which may finally expunge Black's entire system from the K-K canon. Black now experiences serious problems with his queen's bishop and the pawn on d5 – both exposed to attack by the white queen.

Surprisingly in earlier games between the two Ks the inferior 14 ♖b1 had always been played, transposing after 14 ... ♗c6 into the previous game of the present match.

14	...	cd	29
15	♘xd4	15	♗xd4	31

This capture surrenders a useful black unit but it does have the virtue of stabilising the central situation. Furthermore, Kasparov must already have had in mind his freeing pawn sacrifice which he plays three moves later. It should be noted that 15 ... ♘c5 is also possible if Black is striving for a more murky middle-game.

16	ed	15	♘b6	32

If 16 ... ♕b6 not 17 ♘xd5 ♕xb3 18 ♘e7+ ♔h8 19 ab ♖fe8 skewering White's pieces on the e-file, but 17 ♖ab1 maintaining the pressure.

17	a4	24

By far the most forcing continuation.

17	...	♖b8	44
18	a5	31	♘c4!	67

Nobody expected Kasparov to play the humiliatingly passive 18 ... ♘d7, even though White cannot yet cash in his chips with 19 ♘xd5 on account of 19 ... ♕g5 20 ♗f3 ♗a6. Kasparov nearly always prefers activity to material, and the

97

text invests a pawn to liberate his hitherto dormant queen's bishop.

19	♗xc4	52	dc	67
20	♕xc4	52		

A critical position. Black enjoys evident compensation for the pawn, but given the time to consolidate (e.g. by playing d5, ♕d4 and ♖fd1) White will equally evidently be winning.

At this point Kasparov thought for almost half an hour. However, in a TV interview after the game he implied that 'an incorrect queen move' had made life more difficult for him in his task of holding on. Since Black makes one move with his queen and then exchanges, it must be presumed that his next move is the error.

20	...	♕d6!?	92

In many ways a brilliant move, and certainly superior to wild tries such as 20 ... ♕h4, 20 ... ♕g5 or even 20 ... ♕f6. Nevertheless, in spite of the powerful threats Black

introduces with this (... ♗a6/... ♖fc8) it is likely that the most efficient move is 20 ... ♖c8, e.g. 21 ♕b4 ♗a6 and ... ♖c4, or 21 ♕d3 and only now 21 ... ♕d6 22 ♖fc1 ♗a6 23 ♕d2 ♖c4 24 ♘e2 ♕b4. This is a line given by Georgadze and it should establish a draw without too much trauma. Kasparov's choice allows Karpov to trade queens and transpose into an endgame a pawn ahead.

21	♕c5!	75

Karpov avoids 21 ♖fd1 ♖fc8 22 ♕d3 ♕c6 with dual threats against g2 and c3. Also 21 ♖fc1 ♖fd8 22 ♖ab1 ♖bc8 23 ♕b4 ♕xd4 24 ♕xd4 ♖xd4 25 ♖xb7 ♖xc3 26 ♖f1 ♖a4 27 ♖xa7 ♖ca3 is drawing. What now ensues is a long forced sequence.

21	...	♕xc5	107
22	dc	75	♖bc8	107

Not 22 ... ♖fc8? 23 ♖fb1 ♖xc5 24 ♘e4 and the pin on the b-file is lethal.

23	a6	83

23 ♘a4 ♗c6 is too negative. Karpov goes for the much more ambitious plan of winning Black's a7 pawn.

23	...	♗a8	108

Of course not 23 ... ♖xc5? 24 ♘a4.

24	♘b5	93

24 ♖a5 is ludicrously passive.

24	...	♖xc5	113
25	♘xa7	94

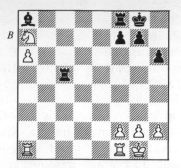

At first glance this position appears desperate for Black, but two key factors come to his rescue: White's extra advanced passed a-pawn is heavily blockaded and, for the moment at least, White's knight on a7 is trapped. In order to salvage the beast White will have to make some concessions. Kasparov now finds and continues to find the very best defence.

Alternatives from the diagram which promise less:

a) 25 ... ♗xg2 26 ♔xg2 ♖a8 27 ♖fb1 ♖xa7 28 ♖b7 ♖a8 29 a7 ♖5c8 30 ♖ab1 and Black is obviously suffering. Restoration of material equilibrium turned out to be less significant than the initiative White was able to seize.

b) 25 ... ♖b8 26 ♖fc1 ♖xc1+ 27 ♖xc1 ♖b6 28 ♖a1 threatening f3 followed by ♖a5 and ♘b5. There is a curious trap here. White has to resist the temptation to win a piece with 28 f3? ♖xa6 29 ♖c8+ ♔h7 30 ♖xa8. Even though he will have

an extra knight it can only be liberated by a long white king march to b6. Meanwhile Black's active rook could easily decimate White's kingside pawns, thus obtaining a simple draw.

25 ... ♗e4! 117

This fine move ensures transposition to the double rook ending from variation 'a' above but with two differences: Black fails to regain material equality, but he does keep sufficient momentum to sustain the blockade of White's a-pawn. If now 26 ♖fe1 ♖a8 27 ♖xe4 ♖xa7 28 h3 ♖c6 29 ♖ea4 and the position has burnt out to a theoretical draw where White can make absolutely no progress. Karpov tries a slightly different tack, leading to a radically similar endgame but not one specifically known to endgame theory – the difference of course is that White has a pawn on the e-file and not the f-file. Logically this should also be a draw, but it was significant that none of the grandmasters in Seville was prepared to stick his neck out and say apodictically that this endgame was an outright draw.

26 f3 100 ♖a8 124

Naturally, 26 ... ♗xf3 would be even worse than 25 ... ♗xg2.

27	fe	102	♖xa7	125
28	♖a4	111	♖c6	126
29	♖fa1	114	♔f8	131
30	♔f2	115	♔e7	132
31	♔e3	113	♔e6	134

32	♖a5	*118*	♖d6	*137*
33	♖1a2	*121*	♖c6	*139*
34	h4	*131*		

The stage is set. White's rooks are bound to the defence of the a-pawn and White's king cannot pass to the queenside to assist the pawn. Thus 34 ♔d4 fails to 34 ... ♖d7+ 35 ♖d5 ♖a7 36 ♖da5 ♖d7+ 37 ♔e3 ♖a7 ad infinitum. Therefore White's only possible theatre of war is the kingside. At some point Karpov must thrust forward his kingside pawns in order to make progress. It would seem that this point has now come, but after a bold sally on move 34 Karpov immediately retreats into his shell and keeps the position stable for adjournment analysis. In fact, it would have been more sensible to push the g-pawn as well before adjournment. It would have been considerably more difficult for Kasparov to have found the correct defence over the board than after hours of analysis.

Karpov delayed his offensive until the second session and when the time came Kasparov and his team (not forgetting the lesson of game 17) had worked out the perfect antidote.

34	...		♖d6	*139*
35	♔f4	*132*	♖b6	*139*
36	♖2a3	*138*	♖c6	*141*
37	♖e5+	*141*	♔f6	*141*
38	♖f5+	*141*	♔e6	*141*
39	♖fa5	*141*	♖b6	*141*
40	♖e5+	*143*		

While Karpov has been busy doing nothing Kasparov has made it to the time control without the need to commit himself to any kind of major defensive decision.

40	...		♔f6	*142*
41	♖ea5	*159*		

The sealed move.

41	...		♔e6	*142*
42	♖a1	*162*	♖c6	*143*
43	♖e5+	*164*	♔f6	*144*
44	♖f5+	*164*	♔e6	*144*
45	♖e5+	*166*	♔f6	
46	♖ea5		♔e6	
47	♖1a2		♖b6	
48	g4			

At last. Kasparov now commits himself to the type of decision which he might have found more arduous before his adjournment analysis.

| 48 | ... | | f6! | |

Black can get into very hot water if he permits g5 taking the f6 square from his king while simultaneously

making e5 available for invasion by a white rook. In that context ... f6 looks natural. The problem is that White, by playing h5, can now fix – and perhaps win – the black g7 pawn. Indeed, Karpov promptly proceeded to do just this, when he should have continued with 49 g5 if he wanted to retain some slim winning prospects. From now on Kasparov quickly and confidently fired off his moves, while Karpov came to look increasingly puzzled.

49	h5		☖c6	
50	☖b2		☖cxa6	
51	☖b6+		☖xb6	
52	☖xa7		☖b1	
53	☖xg7	174	☖f1+	146
54	☗e3		☖e1+	
55	☗f3		☖f1+	
56	☗e2		☖f4	
57	☗e3	178	☗e5!!	147

This is the incredible surprise drawing move.

Karpov clearly had not expected it, and it seems at a glance to lose a rook. On deeper inspection it is a fantastic way to draw.

| 58 | ☖e7+ | 192 | ☗d6 | 148 |

The point. White's rook is also attacked, and the king and pawn endgame is a draw.

59	☖h7		☗e5	
60	☖e7+		☗d6	
61	☖e6+		☗xe6	

Karpov's joke check does not alter the tempo situation for the king and pawn ending.

| 62 | ☗xf4 | 199 | ☗e7 | 150 |

Draw Agreed

If 63 e5 ☗e6 or 63 ☗f5 ☗f7 64 e5 fe 65 ☗xe5 ☗e7, and in spite of his extra pawn White cannot break into the Black fortress.

| Kasparov | ½ 0 ½ 1 0 ½ ½ 1 ½ ½ 1 ½ ½ ½ ½ 0 ½ ½ ½ | 9½ |
| Karpov | ½ 1 ½ 0 1 ½ ½ 0 ½ ½ 0 ½ ½ ½ ½ 1 ½ ½ ½ | 9½ |

101

GAME TWENTY, 4 December

Karpov's defence was ice-cool in tonight's game. It had to be, for he was slammed right in the opening with an inspired sequence by the champion, culminating in a temporary sacrifice of a piece on move 11.

Confident in his prepared shock variation Kasparov was moving quickly, while Karpov was rooted to the board, determinedly seeking to thread his way through the myriad complications which Kasparov had conjured up. As the opening complexities subsided Kasparov emerged into the middlegame with a clear strategic edge, consisting of superior development and greater control of space. But at this critical stage of the battle Karpov demonstrated his extraordinary skill in defence. Time and again he found the only resource to keep his position afloat, and when faced with imminent loss of the game on time he still produced the radical resource 32 ... f5. After this Kasparov's initiative swiftly melted away and the draw came in a level endgame of queens and pawns.

For today's game there had been a tremendous atmosphere of tension and expectation in the teatro. With such greats as Smyslov and Korchnoi fuelling the furious debate in the analysis chamber there was a sense that this was, at long last, Kasparov's mighty push for a breakthrough. But Karpov's defences held and now, just as last year, the title will be decided over the final four games. This time, though, the stakes have been dramatically raised. Whoever wins will wield the sceptre of the chess world for three years to come.

Kasparov-Karpov

Queen's Gambit Declined

1	c4	01	e6	02
2	♘c3	01	d5	02
3	d4	01	♗e7	03
4	♘f3	03	♘f6	03

5	♕c2	03

A remarkable move, which most of the gurus in the press room suspected was probably new. But the editor of the 'flash bulletin' here, Ricardo Montecatine, who must have the Spanish version of 'Every

Game Ever Played' on disk, quickly came up with some theoretical references.

5   ...   0-0   07

Thus, for example, Black can also play 5 ... c5 6 dc ♘a6 (6 ... d4 7 ♘b5 ♘c6 8 ♗f4 looks dangerous) 7 ♗g5 ♕a5 8 e3 ♘xc5 9 ♘d2 dc 10 ♘xc4 ♘d3+ 11 ♗xd3 ♕xg5 12 0-0, Eingorn-Smyslov, USSR 1986. White has a slight edge.

6   ♗g5   03

Re-entering something approaching a main line, the difference being that White's queen is already on c2 and he has not yet played e3.

6   ...   c5   12

There are some alternatives here such as 6 ... ♘bd7 7 e3 h6 8 cd, a piece sacrifice tried in Kasparov-Portisch, OHRA 1986. The intention is 8 ... hg 9 de fe 10 ♘xg5 ♘b6 11 h4 with tremendous compensation in terms of long-range pressure against the black king.

6 ... h6 7 ♗xf6 ♗xf6 8 e4 de 9 ♕xe4 c5 10 0-0-0 would also seem to be something Black should strive to avoid.

7   dc   04   dc   14

Sensibly clearing up the centre and thus increasing his prospects of equality, though at this stage it is doubtful whether Karpov was aware of the analytical storm that was brewing.

8   e4   07   ♕a5   17
9   e5   09   ♘d5   18

10   ♗xc4   09

This capture apparently constitutes a novelty, according to the database of the omniscient Montecatine, who discovered published analysis giving 10 ♗xe7 ♘xe7 11 ♗xc4 ♕xc5 12 ♗d3 ♘g6 13 ♗xg6 hg as equal. The immediate capture is, however, possible due to a subtle point revealed by White's 11th move.

10   ...   ♘xc3   23
11   0-0!   10

Here is the evidently prepared crux of Kasparov's opening variation. Black now has to tread a steady path to reach something less than equality.

11   ...   ♕xc5!   44

Karpov invested a lot of thought in the opening but comes up with ideal defensive moves. There are ways to sink without trace, e.g. 11 ... ♗xg5 12 ♘xg5 g6 13 bc ♕xc5 14 ♕e4 with threats such as ♕h4 exploiting the weakened dark squares around the black king.

Or 11 ... ♘d5 12 ♗xd5 ed 13 ♗xe7 again with dark square domination.

12 ♕xc3 *25*

Now Kasparov thought for some time. 12 ♗xe7 ♕xe7 13 ♕xc3 is also possible but does not radically alter the contours of the situation.

12 ... ♘c6 *59*

Gufeld criticised this and was all for 12 ... b6 to solve the problem of Black's queen's bishop. But after 13 ♗xe7 ♕xe7 14 ♘d4 (with ideas of ♘b5-d6) 14 ... ♗b7 15 ♗b3 ♖c8 16 ♕h3 Black's prospects do not look better than in the game.

13 ♗xe7 *27* **♕xe7** *59*
14 a3 *39*

A refined move which quietly augments his dark square grip. Once again Gufeld proposed the 'improvement' 14 ♖ad1 planning the simple ♖d6 and ♖fd1. Korchnoi countered by suggesting that Black had to trade one pair of rooks, e.g. by 14 ... ♖d8 15 ♗b3 ♖xd1 16 ♖xd1 ♗d7 followed by ... ♖d8, when it is not clear that White can achieve anything.

14 ... ♗d7 *65*

Not a great square for the bishop, so often the problem child of queen pawn openings, but if 14 ... b6 then 15 ♗b5 is very awkward.

15 ♖ac1 *42* **♖fd8** *74*

This position represents a strategic Rubicon for White. Should he attack on the king's flank or the queen's? After immense reflection

Kasparov chooses the latter, but at the close of play he felt that this might have been where he first let his advantage slip.

The major alternative is 16 ♕e3, e.g. 16 ... ♖ac8 17 ♗d3 ♗e8 18 ♖c4. In that case Black has to be wary of combinations based on ♗xh7+, ♖h4+ and ♘g5, with the further threat of ♖h8+ and ♕h3+. If Black plays the cautious 18 ... h6 then 19 ♖fc1 cements White's advantage.

Kasparov's choice gains useful territory for a future endgame but has the drawback of weakening his queenside pawns in the middle-game.

16 b4 *78* **a6** *90*

There was much discussion of 16 ... b5, but then 17 ♗xb5 ♘xb4 18 ♗c4 ♘d5 19 ♗xd5 ed 20 ♕c5 is very much in White's favour. Black also fails to shake off the pressure after 18 ... ♘c6 19 ♗a6 ♖ab8 20 ♖b1. Karpov's plan is much more flexible.

| 17 | ♕e3 | 82 | ♗e8 | 96 |
| 18 | ♗d3 | 89 | ♘a7 | 103 |

This prepares freeing exchanges which White at first seeks to avoid.

19	♗b1	93	♗c6	106
20	♘g5	96	h6	109
21	♘e4	96		

With designs against d6 and f6 if Black is not careful.

| 21 | ... | | ♘b5 | 110 |

A cool reply, intending to parry 22 a4 with 22 ... ♘d4 23 ♘d6 ♕g5, when White has nothing.

| 22 | ♖c4 | 106 | | |

Threatening ♘f6+, so the time has come to liquidate.

| 22 | ... | | ♗xe4 | 116 |
| 23 | ♗xe4 | 108 | | |

Envisaging a slightly advantageous endgame where the white bishop will be superior to Black's knight. If 23 ♕xe4 g6 24 ♕e3 ♔g7? 25 ♖fc1 with a great advantage, but Black simply plays 24 ... ♖ac8 when 25 ♖xc8 ♖xc8 26 ♕xh6 ♘xa3 is fine. Note how any White attempt to switch the action towards the kingside tends to founder on the instability of his pawns on a3 and b4.

23	...		♖ac8	117
24	♖xc8	111	♖xc8	117
25	♖c1	111	♖xc1+	119
26	♕xc1	115	♕d7	119
27	g3	115	b6	121

Normally queen and knight represent a more flexible combination of forces than queen and

bishop – the problem for the queen-bishop duo is that they tend to duplicate functions. This position is an exception and Black must continue to play with the utmost care to avoid losing. Black's difficulty is the lack of a truly stable square for his knight and White's prospects of picking off a queenside pawn. Kasparov believed that he should now have played 28 a4. If 28 ... ♘d4 then 29 ♕d1 pins the knight in unpleasant fashion. If 28 ... ♘c7 the knight is chased back to a more passive location, when White could try 29 a5 or 29 ♕c4. It is doubtful even in this case that White could win against the best defence, but he might have adjourned with an edge and caused overnight suffering to Karpov and his team.

28	♔g2	115	♕d8	119
29	h4	130	a5	128
30	ba	134	ba	128
31	♕c5	134	♘d4	129

Now that the pin motif is no

longer available Black's knight can aspire to its most effective square. Kasparov now proceeds to squeeze on the king's flank.

32 h5 *135* **f5!** *134*

After long thought Karpov finds a heroic defensive resource. If he sits passively with 32 ... ♘f5 then 33 g4 ♘e7 34 ♕d6 is one unpleasant example of what might occur.

The most dangerous line Karpov had to calculate (in time shortage) was 33 ef gf 34 ♔h2 (not 34 ♗g6? ♕a8+) 34 ... f5 35 ♗g2 ♔g7 36 ♕a7+ ♔g8 37 ♕b7 waiting for a black king move, e.g. 37 ... ♔h8 38

♕f7. But now that White's queen no longer attacks the knight on d4 Black can play 38 ... ♕e8 hitting h5, and the whole defensive operation holds together. Recognising that he cannot gain anything by liberating his bishop in this fashion, Kasparov immediately played . . .

33 ♗b7 *135*

This will meet 33 ... ♕b8 with 34 ♕c8+, when the bishop v knight ending still favours White. Karpov's next finesse, however, finally banishes all danger.

33	...		♔f7	142
34	♔h2	139	♕b8	147
35	♕xd4	143		

Not 35 ♗g2 ♕b2.

35	...		♕xb7	147
36	g4	143		

A final try.

36	...		♕f3	148
37	♕d7+	143	♔f8	148

And Kasparov offered a draw which Karpov accepted. Once again, the two stayed on stage for a while to discuss the game.

Kasparov	½ 0 ½ 1 0 ½ ½ 1 ½ ½ 1 ½ ½ ½ ½ 0 ½ ½ ½ ½	10
Karpov	½ 1 ½ 0 1 ½ ½ 0 ½ ½ 0 ½ ½ ½ ½ 1 ½ ½ ½ ½	10

GAME TWENTY-ONE, 7 December

Kasparov inched nearer his goal of 12 points tonight when he held easily with Black. To many observers this seemed a rerun of game 15 but in a minor key, the draw coming much earlier than in that curiously similar encounter.

Karpov decided once again to test Kasparov's favourite Grünfeld Defence and to this end he introduced an innovation on move 14 which varied from his play in game 15. Kasparov was, however, equal to the task and devised a plan which quite neutralised the White initiative, his counterplay culminating in the tactical coup 19 ... ♘d3.

In the press room Smyslov and women's world champion Maya Chiburdanidze both overlooked that this knight leap was possible and had only been analysing knight retreats. This led the two Soviet commentators to the conclusion that Karpov had also overlooked the move, but to us this seems quite incredible, especially considering the long history of d3 knights in K-K games.

In due course Karpov was obliged to sacrifice his rook for the intrusive black knight, but White obtained distinct compensation in the shape of an advanced passed pawn in the centre. With time trouble approaching both players abandoned their winning attempts and acquiesced in a draw by repetition of position on move 28.

This result may be something of a disappointment for Karpov who now has to win one of the final three games to seize the title from his rival. Nevertheless, on the run of play he could perhaps count himself fortunate to escape Black's middlegame initiative. Spassky and Kavalek, two other luminaries recently arrived in Seville (Spassky is here for the second time), felt that if anyone was better it was Black and that Kasparov should perhaps have played on, or at least deferred his aggressive but loosening move 23 ... f5 which brought matters to a crisis by threatening ... f4.

In his post-game TV interview, though, Kasparov seemed content enough with the result, which he considered a logical outcome of the position. Possibly those who felt he should have striven for more have never had a Karpov passed pawn stuck in their entrails.

Karpov-Kasparov
Grünfeld Defence

1	d4	00	♘f6	00
2	c4	00	g6	01
3	♘c3	00	d5	01
4	♘f3	00	♗g7	01
5	♕b3	01	dc	02
6	♕xc4	01	0-0	02
7	e4	01	♘a6	04
8	♗e2	02	c5	05
9	d5	02	e6	05
10	0-0	02	ed	05
11	ed	02	♗f5	06
12	♖d1	04	♖e8	07
13	d6	05	h6	09

14   ♗f4   05

Karpov's new try, varying from the 14 h3 of game 15. At that time we expected 14 ♗f4 to be met by 14 ... g5 or 14 ... ♘h5 harrying the bishop, but Kasparov actually has something much more subtle in mind.

14   ...   ♘d7   15

Proceeding just as he did in game 15, but this almost looks like a tempo loss since White has the aggressive developing move ♗f4 instead of the prudent h3. Nevertheless, Black's armoury is by no means limited to one line of play and Kasparov soon demonstrates that he does not need to rely exclusively on the queenside pawn expansion which was the theme of his counterplay in the stem game.

15	♖d2	11	♘b4	16
16	♕b3	14	♗e6	34
17	♗c4	21	♘b6	62

An excellent and quite unexpected move. It appears that White is forcing events but this refined idea rapidly underscores the fact that White has some highly sensitive weak squares in the central zone – and one of them is d3.

18   ♗xe6   40   ♖xe6   63

At this point White appears to lose the initiative associated with the first move, but it may be that it has already deserted to the other side. The key question is whether White can go in for adventures with 19 ♘b5, e.g. 19 ... ♖e4 20 ♗e3 ♘c4 21 ♗xc5 ♘xd2 22 ♘xd2 ♖e2 23 ♕xb4 (23 ♗xb4 ♕b6) 23 ... a5 24 ♕f4 g5. Opinions differed on this, but the general consensus was that Black had no problems – rather the reverse. Karpov's next move looks naive, since it drives the black knight where it wants to go. But can White improve his position otherwise? If he procrastinates Black may consolidate with ... ♕d7 and reroute the knight via c6 to d4 if prodded, while carelessly playing 'natural' moves can even land White in serious trouble, e.g. 19 ♖ad1? a5!.

Karpov prefers to commit himself to a future exchange sacrifice along the pattern of game 15.

| 19 | a3 | 66 | ♘d3 | 67 |

Clearly the knight is immune on account of ... c4.

| 20 | ♗g3 | 70 | c4 | 70 |
| 21 | ♕c2 | 72 | ♖c8 | 84 |

And not the over-exuberant 21 ... ♘xb2? 22 ♕xb2 ♘a4 23 ♘xa4 ♗xb2 24 ♖xb2 ♕a5 25 ♖b4.

| 22 | ♖ad1 | 83 | ♕d7 | 88 |
| 23 | h4 | 87 | | |

If now 23 ... ♘xb2? 24 ♕xb2 ♘a4 25 ♕b5 wins outright. However, it is not clear that Black's next (which brutally threatens ... f4) is the best. The simple preparatory precaution 23 ... ♔h8 surely deserved preference. There will be time for ... f5 once the black king has vacated the a2-g8 diagonal.

| 23 | ... | | f5 | 105 |
| 24 | ♖xd3 | 103 | | |

Now or never.

24	...		cd	105
25	♕xd3	106	♘c4	122
26	♕d5	112	♘b6	122

Played without hesitation, openly indicating that Black is happy with a draw. If 26 ... ♘xb2 27 ♖e1 ♖e8 28 ♘b5.

| 27 | ♕d3 | 122 | | |

If 27 ♕b3 Karpov feared 27 ... ♕f7, while Kasparov thought 27 ... ♔h7 favoured Black. This emerged from their extensive post-game analysis broadcast to the watching masses via the Intelligent Chess display screens.

| 27 | ... | | ♘c4 | 123 |
| 28 | ♕d5 | 126 | ♘b6 | 123 |

Draw Agreed

| Kasparov | ½ | 0 | ½ | 1 | 0 | ½ | ½ | 1 | ½ | ½ | 1 | ½ | ½ | ½ | ½ | 0 | ½ | ½ | ½ | ½ | ½ | 10½ |
| Karpov | ½ | 1 | ½ | 0 | 1 | ½ | ½ | 0 | ½ | ½ | 0 | ½ | ½ | ½ | ½ | 1 | ½ | ½ | ½ | ½ | ½ | 10½ |

GAME TWENTY-TWO, 11 December

The 22nd game ended in a speedy draw after a mere nineteen moves. This fresh half point brought Kasparov to within one point of retaining his world title. Quite unlike the heroic game 22 of the last match, Kasparov appeared to make no attempt at all to strive for victory. He chose a fairly unusual though essentially tame variation which caused Karpov to think for 36 minutes over his eighth move. Thereafter, however, Karpov swiftly demonstrated complete equality and Kasparov offered the draw on move 19.

So with two games to go, the question still remained if Kasparov might live to regret not striving harder for a knockout.

Kasparov-Karpov
Queen's Gambit Declined

Chief arbiter Gijssen started White's clock and then reset it after a couple of minutes upon learning that Kasparov had been caught in a traffic jam – pretty unusual procedure!

1	c4	00	e6	00
2	♘c3	00	d5	00
3	d4	00	♗e7	01
4	♘f3	06	♘f6	01
5	♗f4	06	0-0	05
6	e3	06	c5	10
7	dc	06	♗xc5	10
8	♖c1	07	♘c6	46
9	cd	07	ed	47

10	♗e2	07	d4	48
11	ed	07	♘xd4	49
12	♘xd4	07	♕xd4	49
13	♕xd4	07	♗xd4	49
14	♘b5	07		

So far the game has been following Kasparov's own analysis in the Yugoslav *Encyclopedia*. He does not, however, assess the position.

14	...		♗b6	50
15	0-0	08	♗e6	53
16	a3	14	♖fd8	65
17	♘d6	24	♖d7	66

This natural move appeared to shock Kasparov.

18	♗b5	50	♖e7	73
19	♖fe1	60	Draw Agreed	

Kasparov	½	0	½	1	0	½	½	1	½	½	1	½	½	½	½	0	½	½	½	½	½	½	**11**
Karpov	½	1	½	0	1	½	½	0	½	½	0	½	½	½	½	1	½	½	½	½	½	½	**11**

110

GAME TWENTY-THREE, 16 December

No sooner had Karpov taken his final time-out before the crucial 23rd game than the situation was complicated by the dramatic intervention of Tofik Dadashev, the Soviet parapsychologist and magician cited by Kasparov as a former supporter, or guru, in his autobiography *Child of Change* and referred to by Karpov in his pre-match press conference.

In an outspoken, brash and overtly self-publicising interview in the latest issue of the German magazine *Der Spiegel*, Dadashev considerably expands on his role in aiding Kasparov during his earlier matches against Karpov. He boldly claims to have predicted key wins and losses in the three earlier matches for the title between the two. His most ambitious claim is – in spite of self-confessedly having no technical knowledge of chess – to have personally formulated Kasparov's strategy for the critical 24th game of the second match, the game which made Kasparov the youngest world champion in the history of chess. Dadashev states that he has no current contact with Kasparov – in fact he appears quite clearly (despite his loud assertions that he supports neither player at the moment) to have switched his allegiance to Karpov. For instance, he adds ominously: "I have given Karpov three pieces of advice for this match. Naturally I cannot yet reveal what this advice is, but if Karpov follows my recommendations he will become world champion again – and he is following them."

Parapsychological or mystical intervention in sporting contests may seem bizarre – the rational tendency is to dismiss such claims as emanating from charlatans or at best from people with an unusual talent to calm frayed nerves or offer moral support. But fear of such goings on and recourse to such methods is quite common in Russia.

In his last game with White Karpov kicked off, strangely, with Kasparov's new favourite 1 c4, perhaps following a parapsychological tip, and still more strangely Kasparov obliged by choosing a fiercely combative pseudo-Grünfeld, instead of a more resilient line such as a Hedgehog or even transposition to the much maligned but still very

111

solid Queen's Gambit Declined. In keeping with the needle nature of this game Karpov strained every nerve trying to win. Kasparov emptied both barrels of tactical tricks straight at Karpov in the opening but the challenger kept control of his nerves and emerged into the middlegame with a clear strategic advantage. However, as time trouble set in for both players Karpov faltered several times and permitted Kasparov to drum up serious counterchances. The adjourned position was still in White's favour but was not the easy technical exercise which Karpov had been enjoying at most earlier stages of the game. However, Kasparov spectacularly and unexpectedly blew himself to smithereens in the second session, despite Karpov's having proceeded in a curiously hesitant fashion when play resumed. Black's structure was riddled with pawn weaknesses, but although Karpov was evidently willing to wound he was just as clearly afraid to strike. On move 49 he started to repeat the position and on move 50 he withdrew his rook from the menacing square e6, deep in the vitals of the Black position, to c6, a less threatening square. As if overcome by a rush of blood to the head at Karpov's passive tactics, Kasparov suddenly went berserk. He quite unnecessarily sacrificed a rook on move 50 – although this was spectacular it was absolutely unsound and Karpov promptly refuted it with a coup with his bishop on move 53. This left Kasparov's position in utter ruins. Everyone was baffled by Kasparov's dramatic self-destruction. After Karpov's dilatory handling of the initial stages of the session Kasparov had virtually pulled the situation round to equality. It was a tragedy for the champion that he could not continue to control his nerves and dig himself in for a long defence instead of experiencing the chessboard equivalent of a nervous breakdown.

Karpov now leads 12-11 with only game 24 left. Kasparov faces the almost impossible task of having to win this one game to save his title. In the century of world championships this feat of winning the last game to save the title and the match has only been performed once before. This was when the German world champion Emanuel Lasker took the dramatic final game against his Austrian rival Karl Schlechter in their contest of 1910. Even that occasion may well have been a sham. It is widely suspected that there existed a secret agreement, which for publicity reasons would only have been made public if it had become relevant, that Schlechter needed to win the match by two points in order to wrest the title from his canny opponent.

Karpov-Kasparov
Grünfeld Defence (by transposition)

1	c4	*00*		

Already a surprise and a cunning psychological trick to use Kasparov's own opening against him.

1	...		c5	*00*
2	♘f3	*00*	♘f6	*00*
3	♘c3	*00*	d5	*00*

Insisting on a Grünfeld, or at least a type of Grünfeld. In such circumstances, with Black requiring a draw, it might have been more sensible to aim for a Hedgehog with ... e6 and ... b6, the chess equivalent of a nuclear fall-out shelter.

4	cd	*00*	♘xd5	*00*
5	d4	*01*	♘xc3	*00*
6	bc	*01*	g6	*01*
7	e3	*02*		

Karpov chooses a solid line but one with aggressive potential for the middlegame.

7	...		♗g7	*01*
8	♗d3	*02*		

In game 12 of his match against Korchnoi at Merano in 1981 Karpov played 8 ♗b5+, but Black equalised comfortably after 8 ... ♘d7.

8	...		0-0	*08*
9	0-0	*03*	♕c7	*08*
10	♖b1	*05*	b6	*09*

Kasparov seems to be taking risks, considering that half a point would have been great for him. The text positively invites White to play ♗e4 at some stage, immediately introducing tactical complications. In Karpov-Timman, Amsterdam 1985, Black continued 10 ... ♘d7 11 e4 e5, which is perhaps more solid. Kasparov must have known of this game and although it ended as a draw he doubtless feared improvements by Karpov.

11	♕e2	*16*		

11 ♗e4 is possible at once and would be parried by 11 ... ♗b7. Karpov first threatens e4 (should Black now try 11 ... ♗b7) and also improves his coordination before carrying out the threat.

11	...		♖d8	*20*
12	♗e4	*34*		

Karpov accepts the tactical challenge. It is doubtful whether he foresaw all the fireworks Kasparov now ignites but Karpov's near infallible strategic instinct must have told him that White would emerge on top.

If now 12 ... ♗b7 13 ♗xb7 ♕xb7 14 dc is already slightly uncomfor-

113

table for Black, even though the position can be handled as a pawn sacrifice. In place of this minimalist approach Kasparov launches out onto something altogether grander – and more of a gamble.

12	...		♗a6	48
13	c4	41	♘c6	48
14	d5	44	f5	48

14 ... ♘a5 15 ♗d3 is miserably passive, so Black has no choice and must counterattack against White's bishop. 15 ♗xf5 gf 16 dc ♕xc6 would give Black a splendid position with two bishops and active play, so White's next is also obligatory.

| 15 | ♗d3 | 65 | e5 | 50 |

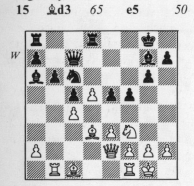

Fantastically imaginative, but should Kasparov really have become entangled in such provocative complexities when he needed a draw so badly? Naturally, 15 ... ♘b4 16 e4 greatly favours White, who blasts open the centre to exploit all of Black's weaknesses, especially the fragile e6 square. What follows is

again forced inasmuch as 16 dc e4 would grant Black all he wants.

16	e4	79	♘d4	51
17	♘xd4	79	cd	51
18	♗g5	86	♖f8	52
19	♖fc1	95	♖ac8	67
20	♗d2	99	♖f7	76

This position with mutual passed pawns looks equal, but it is not. White enjoys the possibility of operating with the dual levers a4-a5 and c5. Black, in contrast, has to endure a siege. He has no real possibility for active play since he has no pawn breaks. The move ... f5, if anything, tends to have undermined Black's own structure.

| 21 | a4 | 105 | fe | 95 |

And not 21 ... ♗f8 22 ef gf 23 ♗xf5 ♖xf5 24 ♕g4+ winning. The text is a necessary positional concession which simply underscores the permanent nature of White's grip.

22	♕xe4	106	♖cf8	101
23	f3	107	♗c8	102
24	a5	113		

Karpov pursues a methodical course, slowly nibbling at Black's queenside pawns. He could have changed tack and gone for a sharp exploitation of his advantage with 24 d6 ♕xd6 25 ♗b4 ♕c7 26 ♗xf8 ♗xf8 when it is, however, hard to break through.

24	...		♗f5	103
25	♕e2	113	♖e8	105
26	♗e4	117	♗f8	106

114

27 ♕d3 *120* **♗c5** *107*

Kasparov has manoeuvred well to repair most of the damage. With cool defence Black should now be able to hold on.

28 ♖a1 *123* **♕d7** *113*
29 ♖e1 *123* **♕c8** *116*
30 ♔h1 *126*

A typical and useful Karpovian safety measure. White evidently does not want his king on the same diagonal as Black's bishop, even though the path is closed at the moment.

30 ... **♖c7** *124*
31 ♖ab1 *128* **♔g7** *124*
32 ♖ec1 *130* **♗xe4** *132*
33 fe *130*

In order to lend permanent protection to the passed pawn on d5.

33 ... **♖f7** *137*
34 ♕g3 *133*

Kasparov now takes a decision which is very difficult to justify. Surely correct here is 34 ... ♕c7, refusing at all costs to destroy his own pawn structure by capturing

on a5. Black would then follow up by playing ... ♖ef8 seizing the f-file as in the game but with the vital difference of a bomb-proof queen's wing.

For the sake of gaining a couple of ultimately insignificant tempi Kasparov now wrecks his queen's wing irrevocably and deprives the bishop on c5 of its sole means of support, the pawn on b6.

34 ... **ba** *137*

Beyond our comprehension, Georgadze in the bulletin actually gives this move an exclamation mark.

35 ♗xa5 *137*

In our view Kasparov is now strategically lost. Black drums up sudden f-file counterplay but it should not be adequate.

35 ... **♖f4** *138*
36 ♖e1 *139* **♕a6** *143*
37 ♗d2 *140*

If 37 ♗c7 ♕f6.

37 ... **♖f7** *143*
38 ♕d3 *144* **♖ef8** *143*

39 h3 *143*

It is vital to make *luft* for the king with Black's major pieces swirling in the vicinity.

39 ... ♖f2 *144*

40 ♖a1 *147* **♛f6** *146*

An improvement would be 40 ... ♛c8 with the immediate threat of 41 ... ♖8f3 demolishing White's position at a stroke. Remember this move – it rears its head again in dramatic fashion. White stays on top after 40 ... ♛c8 but has to waste a move with 41 ♔g1 to repel invaders.

Karpov here sealed his 41st move, and got it wrong.

41 ♖g1? *154*

With Black's major pieces massing round White's king like whirling dervishes it is understandable that Karpov was concerned about the security of his most important piece. However, 41 ♖eb1 is much stronger and would in fact win. Black's kingside attack is still-born and his best riposte may be the desperate 41 ... ♛h4 42 ♗e1 ♛g5 43 ♗xf2 ♖xf2 followed by the rather forlorn attempt ... ♛e3. The problem, and an insuperable one at that, is that White threatens ♗e1-g3 combined with ♖b5 nudging away the blockading bishop on c5. Karpov could, by these means, have reached the desired situation many tempi in advance of the game continuation.

41 ... h5 *47*

What follows – for a while – is a masterly exercise in recovery by Kasparov. His first task is to push a pawn to h4 and prevent White's bishop landing up there.

42 ♖a5 *154* **♛e7** *142*

43 ♖b1 *156* **h4** *148*

44 ♖a6 *163* **♖8f7** *151*

45 ♖c6 *173* **♛f8** *173*

Black falls back in good order. It is considerably more effective in triple major piece scenarios to have the most powerful unit, the queen, backing up the rooks, rather than vice versa.

46 ♖g1 *176*

Karpov starts to play hesitantly but it is not clear how he could improve after the poor sealed move.

46 ... ♗e7 *194*

47 ♖e6 *193* **♔h7** *194*

If now 48 ♖xe5 ♗d6 with great counterplay.

48 ♗e1 *198* **♖f1** *203*

49 ♗d2 *201*

Repeating moves – Kasparov cannot have been playing for a win but he nevertheless avoids repetition and tries to improve his position.

49 ... ♗c5 *204*

With the idea 50 ... ♖xg1+ 51 ♔xg1 ♖f1+ 52 ♛xf1 d3+ winning. Therefore Karpov attacks the bishop to frustrate this knavish trick.

50   Rc6   *202*

Kasparov now has a massive hallucination and commits a blunder that most present believed would cost him the title.

Ironically, White has proceeded in such dilatory fashion that Black could now hold on with 50 ... ♗b4!. If 51 ♗g5 ♗e1 followed by ... ♗g3 tightening the noose around the white king with a probable Black win. If 51 ♗xb4 Rxg1+ 52 ♔xg1 ♕xb4, when White must run for the draw with 53 d6 ♕e1+ 54 ♔h2 Rf1 55 ♕xf1 ♕xf1 56 d7 ♕f4+ etc. The only way for White to play for a win is the incredibly retrograde 51 Ra6 ♗c5 (threat ... Rxg1+ and ... Rf1+ as usual) 52 Raa1 R1f2 and if 53 ♗e1 R2f4. Meanwhile Black always has tactical motifs like ... ♕c8 or ... Rf3 to keep White busy.

Dorfman also gives the move 50

... a5 as satisfactory for Black. White cannot take by 51 ♗xa5 since then the ... Rf3 trick works, White's bishop having been handily deflected from the c1-h6 route. In the meantime White's rook on c6 is cut off from retreating to a1 for defence.

Black's chances appear no worse than White's after either of these suggested improvements. Instead, Kasparov executes the ... Rf3 idea at absolutely the wrong moment and is foiled by a simple bishop move.

50	...	R7f3???	*206*
51	gf	*205*	Rxf3	*208*
52	Rc7+	*205*	♔h8	*206*
53	♗h6!	*205*		

Obvious and crushing.

53	...	Rxd3	*208*
54	♗xf8	*205*	Rxh3+	*208*
55	♔g2	*205*	Rg3+	*208*
56	♔h2	*205*	Rxg1	*208*
57	♗xc5	*207*	d3	*208*

Now capturing Black's rook would allow the d-pawn to queen, but White can win easily by either 58 ♗b4 or 58 ♗e3, preparing to give up the bishop if necessary and promote one of his own passed pawns. Kasparov resigned without waiting for White to play one of these obvious moves.

Black Resigns

Kasparov	½ 0 ½ 1 0 ½ ½ 1 ½ ½ 1 ½ ½ ½ ½ 0 ½ ½ ½ ½ ½ ½ 0	11
Karpov	½ 1 ½ 0 1 ½ ½ 0 ½ ½ 0 ½ ½ ½ ½ 1 ½ ½ ½ ½ ½ ½ 1	12

117

GAME TWENTY-FOUR, 18 December

"I went mad again," was Kasparov's rueful comment on rejoining his shell-shocked seconds after his ghastly loss in game 23. But his mood was quite calm and collected according to Andrew Page, his English business manager and close confidant. The gathering settled down to a game of cards, which considering the circumstances showed commendable *sangfroid*. "After all," Page confided, "Gary is the best player in the world on his rating. In this match he has relied too much on the advice of others, though no one can doubt that his mother has been a tremendous help to him in everything he has achieved, and that he has good friends around him.

"But what he really needs now is to stand on his own feet and accept responsibility for his own decisions, like any other young man growing up in the modern world." Page added that even if Kasparov should lose the final game he had no doubt that he would win the title back in three years time.

After a very slow start to this crucial final game of the battle for supremacy in world chess it appeared that Karpov had every prospect of gaining the half point he required to become champion. Kasparov's opening was quiet and not at all the kind of thing one would expect from a man who had to win at all costs to stay champion.

But as the game wore on Karpov became afflicted by serious time shortage. He was finding it ever more difficult to play his moves at the required speed, even though the position held few apparent dangers for him. On move 30 Kasparov tried a final gamble, offering a pawn sacrifice during Karpov's time shortage. Karpov snatched the pawn but, stunned by the unexpected turn of events, he defended inaccurately and suddenly found himself exposed to a vicious attack. During this hectic phase of the battle Karpov became so short of time that the electronic clocks even indicated he had lost on time forfeit. This was not confirmed by the manual clocks used in the game but at periodic intervals shouting and screaming came from the audience in the adjacent lecture hall who erroneously believed that Karpov had lost on time.

In order to beat off this ferocious last-ditch onslaught Karpov was obliged to shed a pawn himself. He then faced a night of analysis to determine whether the position could be held. Kasparov's extra pawn was balanced by the fact that all the pawns were on the same side of the board. This is a notorious complication when trying to win endgames of this nature. In any case, the stakes riding on this one final position were immense – tenure of the world crown for three years to come and the lion's share of the prize fund of £1.17 million. Grandmaster opinion here at adjournment was divided on whether the position could be won by White, and at his post-match press conference Kasparov himself admitted that before resumption he believed he had only a 50% chance of winning. But he added that "Psychologically Karpov was in despair," and indeed the challenger failed to put up the stiffest resistance in the second session.

So in a miraculous final game Kasparov did it. There was a true sense of history in being present at this decisive 120th championship game between these two great players. Karpov's resignation, which tied the match at 12-12 and left Kasparov as champion, was greeted with a barely credible twenty minute rhythmic ovation from the capacity audience. Meanwhile the two players analysed intently together on the stage, probing each other's thoughts on the adjourned position.

Global interest in this ultimate cliff-hanging clash had been intense. Live TV coverage went out to a potential 300 million viewers around the world, while major coverage of the adjourned position made it to the front page of the *Times*, the *Telegraph* and the *International Herald Tribune*, to name but a few. Tickets in Seville for game 24 had been changing hands at a black market price of 15,000 pesetas (£75), which was over thirty times their face value.

As the players ceased their analysis on the stage of the Lope de Vega the controversial Campomanes entered to declare the contest over. In contrast to the emotion sweeping over the players from the thousand or so spectators, the game's top official was met by jeers – possibly connected with rampant newspaper criticism in Seville alleging wild overspending at the city's expense.

Kasparov-Karpov
English/Reti

		2	♘f3 *00*	♘f6	*02*
		3	g3 *00*		
1	c4 *00*	e6 *00*			

The style of combat inevitably introduced by this reticent move

119

forms an immense contrast to the fierce attempted mating attack launched by Karpov when he had to win at all costs in game 24 from K-K II, Moscow 1985. Kasparov goes instead for the most micro-scopic of enduring edges, hoping to subject Karpov's understandably fragile nerves to endless torture.

3	...		d5	05
4	b3	00	♗e7	12
5	♗g2	00	0-0	15

The fact that Karpov had taken fifteen minutes over these obvious and simple moves indicates the tension pressing on him.

6	0-0	00	b6	21
7	♗b2	00	♗b7	21
8	e3	05		

White's opening is an old favour-ite of Kasparov's mentor Botvinnik, although the symmetrical type of position to which it tends offers few and rarefied winning prospects. This, however, was all part of Kasparov's game strategy – in an all-or-nothing clash such as this there has to be some element of gamble. Kasparov gambled (unlike Karpov in 1985) on slow pressure rather than a death-or-glory assault.

8	...		♘bd7	36

Karpov continues to play at a snail's pace. It would have been more sensible to play natural moves quickly and save up energy for the middlegame shoot-out.

9	♘c3	19	♘e4	47

10	♘e2	23		

A fascinating decision. Kasparov wants to avoid the exchange of knights – complex strategic pieces – but does not care about the exchange of bishops which now occurs by force. Of course, any kind of exchange would be manna to Karpov, who so desperately craved a draw.

The normal move is 10 ♕e2, when Botvinnik-Stahlberg, Moscow 1956, continued (by trans-position) 10 ... a5 11 ♖fd1 ♗f6 12 d4, with some advantage to White.

10	...		a5	49
11	d3	40		

Kasparov begins to catch up on clock time.

11	...		♗f6	61
12	♕c2	49	♗xb2	63
13	♕xb2	50	♘d6	64
14	cd	51	♗xd5	69

This way of recapturing avoids any possible weakness in the Black central pawn structure. White could now try 15 ♘f4 ♗b7 16 ♘h5

120

but 16 ... f6 offers a firm defence.

15 d4 *86* **c5** *86*

Times were now level, and Karpov's last move appears to level the position too. Any slight danger emanating from a potentially backward c-pawn is efficiently eradicated.

16 ♖fd1 *86* **♖c8** *107*
17 ♘f4 *101* **♗xf3** *113*

A favourite Karpov trade when there are no targets along the h1-a8 diagonal. White's bishop is nominally superior to one black knight but it is hard to prove anything.

18 ♗xf3 *101* **♕e7** *113*
19 ♖ac1 *124* **♖fd8** *114*
20 dc *125* **♘xc5** *115*

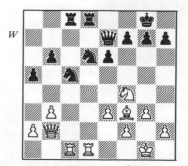

Black's position appears perfectly developed and coordinated – and Karpov even has more time in hand on the clock. Nevertheless, Kasparov's next move, a very fine one indeed, maintains just that slight nagging edge he has been nurturing throughout the game.

21 b4! *126* **ab** *129*

The time consumed indicates that Karpov was becoming unhappy. If, for example, 21 ... ♘ce4 22 ♖xc8 ♖xc8 23 ♕d4 winning material. What he plays permits a sensitive point to develop on b6.

22 ♕xb4 *127* **♕a7** *129*
23 a3 *127* **♘f5** *134*
24 ♖b1 *128* **♖xd1+** *137*

To deflect White's remaining rook away from the attack against b6.

25 ♖xd1 *130* **♕c7** *139*
26 ♘d3 *134* **h6** *142*

Around here Karpov starts to lose the threat of the game. He avoids what might be considered a natural exchanging sequence – 26 ... ♘xd3 27 ♖xd3 ♖d8 28 ♖b3 – and soon he finds his knights stumbling over each other trying to find secure posts.

27 ♖c1 *136*

Introducing an annoying pin motif. There is also the thought that exchanges on c5 in the future may cede White a passed a-pawn promoting on a square covered by White's bishop. Karpov had to cope with all this with about seven minutes on his clock for thirteen moves.

27 ... **♘e7** *144*
28 ♕b5 *137* **♘f5** *146*

Black is evidently unable to keep his knights on a tight rein, as Gufeld wryly observed.

29 a4 *141*

Preparing to undermine the c5 knight with the thrust a5.

29 ... ♘d6 *147*
30 ♕b1 *141* **♕a7** *148*

Two minutes left for Black to reach move 40.

31 ♘e5!? *141*

In the time trouble crisis Kasparov unleashes one of his sudden whiplash attacks. One might have expected exchanges on c5, to create a passed a-pawn. Objectively that would be correct but Kasparov senses that his true chances lie in direct violence against Black's king. Black cannot play 31 ... ♕xa4 32 ♕xb6, so he grabs the pawn with his knight – in a way suggestive of lack of belief in Kasparov's sacrifice.

31 ... ♘xa4 *149*
32 ♖xc8+ *141* ♘xc8 *149*
33 ♕d1 *142*

The point of the sacrifice. White's forces are suddenly concentrated in the direction of Black's king. The defence is evidently hamstrung

by the unstable location of Black's knight on a4. Ironically, however, it is just this knight which should now leap back into the fray with 33 ... ♘c5!. If 34 ♕d8+ ♔h7 35 ♕xc8 then 35 ... ♕a1+, suddenly possible since the knight move has cleared the a-file, regains the piece.

Kasparov later told us that he should, in fact, have played 33 ♕b5 ♘a6 34 ♕c6 to keep up the pressure legitimately.

33 ... ♘e7 *149*

Karpov hesitated, in virtual panic, before finally playing this. No one could believe that he had not lost on time. The concluding moves were fired out in a frantic rush. Kasparov's bluff had worked to the extent that White could still press for a win.

34 ♕d8+ *142*

The immediate 34 ♗h5 is tempting, but at worst Black escapes with 34 ... ♘c5 35 ♗xf7+ ♔h7, when White's onslaught is not yet decisive. 34 ... g6 35 ♕d8+ ♔h7 may also survive, but not 35 ... ♔g7 36 ♘d7 ♘g8 37 ♕f8+ ♔h8 38 ♘f6 winning.

34 ... ♔h7 *149*
35 ♘xf7 *143*

Kasparov does well to avoid attractive adventures during time trouble, concentrating instead on adjourning with an advantage. So often players blow a clear plus by chasing something bigger but more elusive. Here, for example, 35 ♘d7 fails to 35 ... ♘g8, while 35 ♗h5 ♘c5 (threat 36 ... ♕a1+) 36 ♘xf7 ♘g8 allows Black to reorganise his lines of defence.

| 35 | ... | ♘g6 | *149* |

In absolutely desperate time trouble Karpov, to his enormous credit, finds an ice-cool defence.

| 36 | ♕e8 | *144* | ♕e7 | *149* |
| 37 | ♕xa4 | *144* |

Kasparov's advantage translates into an extra pawn, since b6 is doomed.

37	...	♕xf7	*147*
38	♗e4	*144*	♔g8	*149*
39	♕b5	*145*	♘f8	*149*
40	♕xb6	*145*	♕f6	*149*

. . . and Karpov made the time control. He also made one more move just to be ultra-sure.

| 41 | ♕b5 | *147* | ♕e7 | *149* |

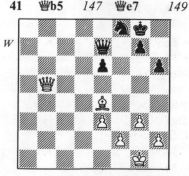

And Kasparov sealed his 42nd move. This adjourned position, flashed overnight to millions of chess lovers around the planet, is destined to become one of the classics, in the same league as the adjourned position from game 34 of Alekhine-Capablanca, 1927, or the adjournment of Botvinnik-Bronstein, game 23 of their 1951 match.

| 42 | ♔g2 | *160* |

A non-committal move, since Kasparov could not be sure without analysis whether White should venture on h4 or not.

| 42 | ... | g6 | *149* |

Sooner or later this will be necessary. When White does play h4 (which is in fact the right approach) Black must stop the pawn advancing to h5. If Black omits ... g6 then White's h5 will cause death by strangulation.

| 43 | ♕a5 | *166* |

White's advantage will not run away. Kasparov tries at first a little probing to see what Karpov's intentions are.

| 43 | ... | ♕g7 | *152* |
| 44 | ♕c5 | *167* | ♕f7 | *154* |

Queen oscillation – so far, so good.

| 45 | h4 | *170* | h5? | *154* |

An unpardonable error after adjournment analysis. Karpov is obsessed (as in game 8) with digging himself into a fortress – it is a prime example of a bunker mentality syndrome. But after this move (Kasparov said to us: "I could not believe my eyes") Black's kingside pawns are eternally fixed on vulnerable light squares. Hence Black is doomed to loss after virtually any queen exchange. But White's queen soon becomes so powerful on the open board that avoidance of the queen trade is equally terminal.

Black's only chance here is to stay flexible – if anything risk playing ... g5 at some point, when White's best reply would be h5. Kasparov and Karpov analysed such variations together at great length after the game. The general conclusion was that White should still win, but there are a myriad technical difficulties. After the text Kasparov wins by force in an artistic process utilising zugzwang motifs.

46	♕c6	178	♕e7	161
47	♗d3	181	♕f7	161
48	♕d6	188	♔g7	164
49	e4	190		

A key component of the winning plan. This pawn must come to e5 to increase White's control of space.

49	...		♔g8	165

50	♗c4	196	♔g7	167
51	♕e5+	199	♔g8	169
52	♕d6	201	♔g7	169

Karpov marks time. What else can he do?

53	♗b5	204	♔g8	171
54	♗c6	204		

This position we had reached ourselves in our own overnight investigation of the adjourned position. Our conclusion was that White should be able to win, but in our analysis the black h-pawn had stayed back on the superior defensive square h6. What transpires in the game is much worse.

54	...		♕a7	194
55	♕b4	205	♕c7	198
56	♕b7	205		

Simultaneously making it to the second time control and offering a trade of queens which Black cannot possibly accept.

56	...		♕d8	198
57	e5!	216		

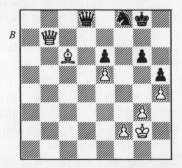

The winning move. Black is now in total zugzwang. Karpov's agony became painfully clear, almost in slow motion as he sat for 45 minutes, desperately thinking of a reply – 45 minutes in which the title ebbed inexorably away from him.

If now 57 ... ♔h8 58 ♕f7 wins, or 57 ... ♕d3 58 ♗e8 ♕f5 59 ♕f3 forcing the fatal queen trade. Finally, 57 ... g5 58 hg ♕xg5 59 ♗e8 ♕f5 60 ♕f3 with the same effect. Karpov finds the only way to offer (brief) resistance.

57	...		♕a5	243
58	♗e8	217	♕c5	243
59	♕f7+	219		

This penetration is decisive.

| 59 | ... | | ♔h8 | 243 |
| 60 | ♗a4 | 220 | | |

The white bishop manoeuvres around until a black pawn drops off.

| 60 | ... | | ♕d5+ | 246 |
| 61 | ♔h2 | 222 | ♕c5 | 246 |

The queen is shackled to the defence of the f8 knight – another 'witness for the prosecution' as in game 8.

62	♗b3	224	♕c8	247
63	♗d1	225	♕c5	248
64	♔g2	226	**Resigns**	

In the final position, one of the most important and historic in the pageant of world championship battles, White's bishop inevitably comes to e4 and starts consuming black pawns.

For those interested in numerology, Karpov resigned on the symbolic 64th move, significant for several reasons. It is, of course, 8 x 8, the number of squares on the chessboard. Additionally and curiously, Kasparov has a very high score of eight wins, six draws and just one loss in games from world championships that are multiples of 8, including two (game 24 in 1985 and this game) which won the world championship for him.

By his resignation Karpov thus conceded to Kasparov the right to retain the world title for a further three years. Kasparov told us later that night he considered this the best game of the match.

| Kasparov | ½ 0 ½ 1 0 ½ ½ 1 ½ ½ 1 ½ ½ ½ ½ 0 ½ ½ ½ ½ ½ ½ 0 1 | 12 |
| Karpov | ½ 1 ½ 0 1 ½ ½ 0 ½ ½ 0 ½ ½ ½ ½ 1 ½ ½ ½ ½ ½ ½ 1 0 | 12 |

Conclusion

It was the best of matches, it was the worst of matches. There were insipid draws. There were fine wins. There were blunders that would have shamed a coffee-house player. There were passages of complexity and brilliance that will be remembered for years to come. Above all there was a cliff-hanging ending which put the story on the front pages around the world.

In the opening phase Karpov showed that his challenge was no mere formality. After five games, three of which were decisive, he was leading 3-2. But Kasparov then seemed to regain his confidence. He equalised in game 8 and after Karpov's horrific blunder in game 11 it was the champion who had a lead of one point. Needing only a tie to retain his title, Kasparov reverted to the stalling tactics which had led to the 'Moscow marathon' of 48 games. During this lacklustre phase of the match Karpov managed to catch up by a well-judged win in game 16. But with a further succession of draws and only two games to go it looked as though Kasparov would hang on. Then, out of the blue, came the dramatic conclusion to it all. In game 23 Kasparov seemed to have recovered from a dubious position, but then he produced the gaffe which most people thought would cost him his title. However, Kasparov was reserving his best performance for the final game. After a quiet start, during which Karpov fell behind on the clock, he managed to conjure up sufficient complications to bamboozle the challenger in his time pressure. The champion's superb endgame technique enabled him to convert a problematical adjourned position into a win.

Although Karpov stumbled at the final fence, it was his reputation rather than the champion's that was enhanced by this match. He had started as underdog and yet managed to draw the match, giving the champion a massive fright in the process. He deserves the title of vice-champion (or even, in Gufeld's opinion, co-champion!) and few doubt that it is he who will again confront Kasparov in 1990.

After 120 championship games spread over four matches in only three years, Kasparov now has three years as the undisputed champion. Gone, as he said with evident relief at the prizegiving ceremony at the end of the match, are the struggles to win the full right to be champion. With his new security he must now decide how much of his abundant energy to devote to his self-appointed role of protector of those who oppose the way FIDE is currently run, and how much to actually playing the game of which he established himself champion in the Showdown in Seville.